A Practitioner's
Approach and Interpretation
of
The Party Wall etc. Act 1996

A Practitioner's

Approach And Interpretation

of

The Party Wall etc. Act 1996

PHILIP ANTINO

To order additional copies of this book, contact:
Xlibris Corporation
0-800-644-6988
www.xlibrispublishing.co.uk
Orders@xlibrispublishing.co.uk
304889

Contents

Table Of References...13
Table Of Cases 15
List of Figures 17
The Author 19
Acknowledgments..21

Chapter 1		The Party Wall etc. Act 1996....................................23
	1.1	Introduction 23
	1.2	An Overview...26
	1.3	Vocabulary 29
	1.4	Agreements (Outside the Act) 31
		1.4.1 Agreements in lieu of Notice..........31
		1.4.2 Agreements subsequent to Notice....32
		1.4.3 Agreements to regularise unlawful works 32
		1.4.4 Agreements relating to variations...32
	1.5	Jurisdiction..33
	1.6	Irregularities and Estoppel............................35
	1.7	Technology 36
	1.8	Policing the Act 37
	1.9	Summary..38

Chapter 2		Definitions..39
	2.1	Introduction 39
	2.2	Adjoining Owner and Adjoining Occupier......40
	2.3	Building Owner 40
	2.4	Owner 42
	2.5	Foundation...44

	2.6	Special Foundations	45
	2.7	Party Fence Wall	47
	2.8	Party Structure	48
	2.9	Party Wall	50
	2.10	Surveyor	57
	2.11	Appointing Officer	58
	2.12	Supplemental Definitions	59
	2.13	Summary	61

Chapter 3   Section 1—Construction and repair of walls on the line of junction ... 62

	3.1	Introduction	62
	3.2	Line of Junction works	62
	3.3	Service of Notice	64
	3.4	Adjoining Owner(s) consent	64
	3.5	Adjoining Owner(s) non-consent	65
	3.6	On the line of junction	66
	3.7	Projecting foundations	71
	3.8	Compensation for projecting foundations	72
	3.9	Disputes under section 1	74
	3.10	Summary	75

Chapter 4   Section 2—Boundary Wall, Party Fence Wall or external wall of a building ... 76

	4.1	Introduction	76
	4.2	Application	76
	4.3	Owners Rights	77
		4.3.1	Repairs to the Party wall	79
		4.3.2	Partitions	80
		4.3.3	Connections	81
		4.3.4	Reconstruction	81
		4.3.5	Penetrating the wall	82
		4.3.6	Cutting away from the party wall	85

	4.3.7	Cutting away overhanging elements .. 86
	4.3.8	Weathering between abutting structures.. 88
	4.3.9	Supplemental works 88
	4.3.10	Change of use 89
	4.3.11	Demolition and reconstruction 89
	4.3.12	Exposure 90
4.4	Chimneys and flues 91
4.5	Liabilities and obligations under (2)(e) 92
4.6	Damage under 2)(f) (g) or (h).......................... 93
4.7	Damage under 2)(j).. 93
4.8	Parapet walls.. 93
4.9	Deemed statutory compliance 94
4.10	Summary.. 95

Chapter 5	Section 3—Party Structure Notices............................. 97
5.1	Introduction 97
5.2	Building Owners details and proposed works . 97
5.3	Statutory notice and due diligence................... 98
5.4	Lawful commencement without notice 100
5.5	Summary.. 101

Chapter 6	Section 4—Counter Notices.. 103
6.1	Introduction 103
6.2	Counter notice... 103
6.3	Reasonable notice 104
6.4	Unreasonable requests 105
6.5	Summary.. 106

Chapter 7	Section 5—Response to a Notice 107
7.1	Introduction 107
7.2	Response to a notice 107
7.3	Summary.. 108

Chapter 8   Section 6—Excavations 109

     8.1   Introduction 109

     8.2   Application of three meter notice 109

     8.3   Application of six meter notice 111

     8.4   Preventative Operations 115

     8.5   Definition 115

     8.6   Reasonable Notice 116

     8.7   Drawings, plans and sections 117

     8.8   Dissent 118

     8.9   Statutory notice and due diligence 118

     8.10   Amended drawings, plans and sections 120

     8.11   Injury and loss 120

     8.12   Summary 121

Chapter 9   Section 7—Inconvenience and Compensation 123

     9.1   Introduction 123

     9.2   Unnecessary inconvenience 123

     9.3   Loss and damage 125

     9.4   Maintaining security 127

     9.5   Special foundations 128

     9.6   Statutory approvals 129

         9.6.1   Permitted Development 130

     9.7   Summary 131

Chapter 10   Section 8—Access Rights 133

     10.1   Introduction 133

     10.2   Achieving lawful access 133

     10.3   Forced access 135

     10.4   Access without notice 136

     10.5   Reasonable notice 137

     10.6   Surveyors access 137

     10.7   Emergency access 138

     10.8   Schedule of Condition 139

     10.9   Summary 140

Chapter 11   Section 9—Easements of Light and/or in relation to a
              party wall.. 141
              11.1   Introduction 141
              11.2   Interference of easements............................. 142
              11.3   Right of Light 144
              11.4   Right of Way.. 145
              11.5   Right of Support 146
              11.6   Transferring an obligation to support 148
              11.7   Drainage Rights 151
              11.8   Weather Protection....................................... 151
              11.9   Rights to Repair 152
              11.10   Summary... 152

Chapter 12   Section 10—Dispute Resolution Procedures 154
              12.1   Introduction 154
              12.2   Appointment of the surveyor(s).................... 154
                      12.2.1   Selection of a Third surveyor 156
              12.3   Once appointed always appointed 157
              12.4   Conditional Appointments............................ 159
              12.5   Agreed surveyors failure to Act.................... 160
              12.6   Failure to appoint a surveyor........................ 161
              12.7   Death or incapable.. 162
              12.8   Refusal to Act 163
              12.9   Neglect to Act 164
              12.11   Third surveyors failure to act....................... 166
              12.12   The Party Wall award 168
                      12.12.1   Interim Inspections 169
                      12.12.2   Retrospective Awards 170
                      12.12.3   Anticipated Awards...................... 171
                      12.12.4   Third Surveyor Award 172
                      12.12.5   Addendum Awards........................ 174
              12.13   Third surveyor referrals................................ 174
              12.14   Determination 175
              12.15   Reasonable costs.. 177

12.16   Service of the award 180

12.17   Service of the Third Surveyors award 181

12.18   The awards jurisdiction 182

12.19   Appeals Procedure 182

12.20   Summary 184

Chapter 13   Section 11—Expenses 186

13.1   Introduction 186

13.2   Liability to pay 186

13.3   Use, defect, and repair 187

13.4   Proportional use and costs 188

13.5   Proportional disturbance and inconvenience . 189

13.6   Retaining the height of the wall 190

13.7   Cash Settlement 191

13.8   Adjoining Owners liability to costs 192

13.9   Special Foundations with Consent 192

13.10   Benefit in Kind 193

13.11   Summary 194

Chapter 14   Section 12—Security of Expenses 195

14.1   Introduction 195

14.2   Adjoining Owners Security 195

14.3   Building owner's security 197

14.4   Adjoining Owners Request for building works .. 198

14.5   Summary 199

Chapter 15   Section 13—Expenses 200

15.1   Introduction 200

15.2   Claiming expenses for works 200

15.3   Challenging reasonableness of expenses 201

15.4   Summary 202

Chapter 16		Adjoining Owners account	203
	16.1	Introduction	203
	16.2	Adjoining Owners liabilities	203
	16.3	Explanation	203
	15.4	Summary	204
Chapter 17		Section 15—Miscellaneous (service of notices etc)	205
	17.1	Introduction	205
	17.2	Service	205
	17.3	Adjoining Owner(s) identity	207
	17.4	Summary	208
Chapter 18		Section 16—Offences	209
	18.1	Introduction	209
	18.2	Obstruction	209
	18.3	Hindrance	210
	18.4	Conviction	211
	18.5	Summary	211
Chapter 19		Section 17—Recovery of Expenses	212
	19.1	Introduction	212
	19.2	Magistrates Court	212
		19.2.1 The Procedure	213
		19.2.2 Costs	214
		19.2.3 Deed of Assignment	215
	19.3	Summary	215
Chapter 20		Section 18—Exclusions	216
	20.1	Introduction	216
	20.2	Barrister's exclusion	216
	20.3	Summary	217

Chapter 21   Section 19—Inclusions 218
              21.1   Introduction 218
              21.2   Queen Elizabeth II 218
              21.3   Duchy of Lancaster and Cornwall 219
              21.4   Summary 219

Chapter 22   Basements 220
              22.1   Introduction 220
              22.2   Wall or Foundation 220
              22.3   Linkage 222
              22.4   Summary 223

Chapter 23   Specimen Documents 224
              23.1   Proposed Letter of Surveyors Appointment.... 224
              23.2   Section 1 Line of Junction 225
              22.3   Party Structure Notice 227
              23.4   Notices—Acknowledgement of
                      Party Structure Notice 229
              23.6   Acknowledgement of 3m/6m Notice 232
              23.7   Draft Award Agreed Surveyor 234
              23.8   Appointed Award 239
              23.9   Service of an Award Letter 245
              23.10   Security of expenses letter 247
              23.11   Referral to Third Surveyor 248
              23.12   Special Foundations Letter 250
              23.13   Informing the Third Surveyor 251
              23.14   Checklist 252

Table Of References

Ainsworth, R., *Differences of Opinion Interpreting Section 1*, Structural Survey Vol. 18 No 5 2000 pp. 213-217.

Antino, P. *Using the Party Wall etc. Act 1996 to gain access to a neighbouring property'* Emerald Group Publishing Limited, Structural Survey, Journal of Building Pathology and Refurbishment, Vol. 29 issue No 3 2011 pp. 210-220.

Bickford-Smith, S. and Sydenham, C. 2nd Ed, (2004) *"Party Walls Law and Practice"*, Jordan Publishing Ltd.

Bickford-Smith, S. and Sydenham, C. 3rd Ed, (2009) *"Party Walls Law and Practice"*, Jordan Publishing Ltd.

Birkinshaw, R. & Parrett, M. (2003) *"Diagnosing Damp"* RICS Business Services Ltd, P.79

Carr, P. & Turner, A. (2011) *'Stones Justices Manual'* Butterworths.

Chynoweth, P. (2000) *Invalid Party Wall Awards and How to Avoid Them* Structural Survey Volume 18 No. 4

Chynoweth, P. *Impartiality in the Party Wall Surveyor* (2001) 17 Const. L.J. No. 2 Copyright Sweet & Maxwell Limited and contributors.

Chynoweth, P. *Making Sense of the Party Wall Legislation: Still No Easy Task* Structural Survey Volume 20 No. 1 2002.

Chynoweth, P. (2003) *'The Party Wall Case Book,'* Blackwell Publishing Ltd.

Chynoweth, P. (2004)*The Scope for Agreement in Statutory Party Wall Procedures* 20 Const. L.J. No. 6 © Sweet & Maxwell Limited and contributors.

Dickinson, P.R. & Thornton, N. (2004) *"Cracking and Building Movement"* RICS Business Services Ltd.

Gaunt, J. Q.C. and Morgan, P. C.C. (2002) *"Gale on Easements"* 7th Edition Sweet & Maxwell Ltd.

Son, L.H. & Yuen, G.C.S. (1993) *"Building Maintenance Technology"* The Macmillan Press Limited.

The Pyramus & Thisbe Club *"The Party Wall Act explained: A Commentary on the Party Wall etc. Act 1996"* The Pyramus & Thisbe Club.

Wood, D. Chynoweth, P. Adshead, A. and Mason, J. (2011) *"Law and the Built Environment"* Wiley-Blackwell.

Table Of Cases

Adams v Marlebone Borough Council [1907] 2 KB 822

Bansal v Myers [2007] Romford County Court Unreported

CA Webber (Transport) Ltd v Railtrack Plc [2003] EWCA C iv 1167

Car-Saunder v Dick McNeil Associates Ltd [1986] 1 WLR 922

Chandler v Thompson (1811) 3 Camp. 80

Chartered Society of Physiotherapy v Simmons

Church Smiles [1995] 1 EGLR

Colls v Holmes and Colonial Stores (1894) 3 Ch. 659

Crosby v Alhambra Co Ltd [1907] 1 Ch 295

Crowley v Rushmore Borough Council [2010] EWHC 2237

Cubit v Porter (1828) 8 B. & C. 257

Dalton v Angus (1881) 6 APP.CAS 740 at 792

Davies & Sleep v Wise [2006] Barnet County Court

Drury v Army & Navy Auxiliary Cooperative Supply Ltd (1896) 2 QB 271

Duke of Westminster v Guild [1985] 1 Q.B. 688 at 700E

Emms v Polya [1973] 227 EG 1659

Frances Holland School v Wassef [2001] 2 EGLR

Freetown Ltd v Assethold Ltd [2012] EWHC 1351 (QB)

Garritt v Sharp (1835) 3.A & E.

Goodhart v Hyett (1884) 25 Ch.D. 182

Gyle-Thompson v Wall Street (Properties) Ltd 1 WLR 123 [1974] 1 ALL ER 295

James v Dods (1834) 2 Cr. & M.266

Jones v Pritchard [1908] 1 Ch. 630

Jones & Lovegrove v Ruth & Ruth [2012] EWHC 1538 and in the Court of Appeal [2011]

Hobbs, Hart & Co v Grover [1899] No. 1 Ch 11

Kaye v Lawrence [2010] EWHC 2678 TCC

Leadbetter v Marylebone Corporation [No. 1] [1904] 2 KB 893

Leadbetter v Marylebone Corporation [No. 2] [1904] 2 KB 893

Lehmann v Herman [1993] 1 EGLR 172

Lemaitre v Davis (1881) 19 Ch.D. 281

Loost v Kremer [1997] West London County Court 12 May (Unreported)

Louis v Sadiq [1997] 1 EGLR 136; (1998) 59 Con LR 127

Matts v Hawkins (1813) 5 Taunt 20.

Manu v Euroview Investments Ltd [2008] 1 EGLR 165

Methuen-Campbell v Walters [1979] (1 QB 525 CA)

Midland Bank plc v Bardgrove Property Services Ltd [1991] 2 EGLR 283

Onigbanjo, A. v Mr & Mrs Pearson [2008] The Mayors and City of London Court

Patsalidies v Foye (2002) [unreported] HHJ RICH QC 29th October 2002]

Phipps v Pears [1964] 2 WLR 996

Prudential Assurance Co Ltd v Waterloo Real Estate Inc (1999) 2 EGLR 85

Rees v Skerrett [2001] 1 WLR 1541

Reeves v Blake [2009] EWCA C iv 611 P.14

Sachs v Jones [1925] AER 514

Selby v Whitbread & Co [1917] 1 KB 736

Sunsaid Property Company Ltd v Omenaka & Omenaka

Spiers and Son Ltd v Troup (1915) 84 LJKB 1986

Standard Bank of British and South America v Stokes (1878) L.R 9 Ch.D

Thurrock Grays & Tilbury Joint Sewage Board v E.J. & W. Goldsmith (1914) 79 J.P.17

Watson v Gray (1880) 14 Ch.D 192 at 194

Western v Arnold (1873) 8 Ch A pp 1084.

Woodhouse v Consolidated Property Corp 1993, 1 EGLR 174

Zissis v Lukomski & Carter [2006] EWCA C iv 341

List of Figures

Illustrations by Alison Exton

Figure 1 & 2	Projecting and Special Foundations
Figure 3, 4 & 5	Line of Junction
Figure 6	Party Structure Notice
Figure 7, 8 & 9	Type (a) party wall
Figure 10 & 11	Type (a) party wall
Figure 12 & 13	Type (b) party wall
Figure 14	Type (b) party wall
Figure 15	Easements
Figure 16	Easements
Figure 17	3m Excavations
Figure 18	6m Excavations
Figure 19	Obligations to Support
Figure 20	Substituted means of Support
Figure 21	Maintaining obligation to Support
Figure 22	Basement special foundations

The Author

Philip Antino is the managing director of APA property Services Ltd and currently just over three years into his PhD on "Professional Interpretation in the Built Environment Professions: A case study of conflicting interpretations of the Party Wall etc. Act 1996 by Surveyors in England and Wales". However, Philip is not an academic looking at the world of party wall surveyors through a rose tinted bowl but a practicing "new school" party wall surveyor.

Philip has published several papers in leading journals on this subject and has assisted in blowing away the cobwebs that surround the myths that exist within the world of party wall surveyors interpretation of the Act. His most notable success is the decision in Bansal v Myers where Philip's interpretation of the surveyor(s) duty to determine costs should not involve the owner(s). However, this decision is a county court judgement and unfortunately not a legal precedent. Although, this case is relied upon and quoted in other leading textbooks on the law and practice of the Party Wall Act it sets an important benchmark.

Philip has lectured extensively on the subject and actively participates in the promotion of good party wall surveying practices. One of the most frustrating activities that the party wall surveyor must undertake is the production and management of the vast amount of documentation that is generated under the Act. The accuracy of these documents will establish the party wall surveyor(s) jurisdiction, make one mistake and everything may be deemed invalid. To remove the drudgery and time involved in managing this process Philip has developed a party wall software programme which virtually eliminates any possibility of human error. This software programme is becoming widely accepted throughout the party wall surveying community.

Acknowledgments

Where does one start when so many people have contributed directly or indirectly to the production of this book. I suppose I should start at the beginning and acknowledge all of my appointing owner(s) and/or the surveyors that have selected me as the Third surveyor, without which my experiences as a party wall surveyor would never have exposed me to the complex issues that I have had to deal with over the past 15 years. Irrespective of whether my opinions and interpretations have clashed with surveyors is irrelevant, every experience leads me to continually assess and evaluate how I interpret and apply the Act and for those opportunities alone I am eternally grateful.

Of course the production of this manuscript would not have been possible without the assistance of my office manager Nicola Bambridge and senior secretary Francesca Antino who have patiently typed and re-typed the manuscript as I have adjusted, amended, altered and in some instances simply scrapped whole sections to start again.

Last and certainly not least I would like to thank my eternally patient family and friends for their support and understanding for all the missed weekends, evenings, and social events whilst I worked into the early hours in producing what I hope is a pragmatic and sensible explanation of my interpretation and application of the Act.

Chapter 1   The Party Wall etc. Act 1996

1.1   Introduction

When I first expressed a desire to write about *"The Party wall etc. Act 1996"* I received a mixed reception from my contemporaries; some thought I was mad given the number of existing titles already written on the subject, others thought it was an excellent idea. In fact it was nearly two years and due to the conduct of certain surveyors approaches to interpreting the Act that I decided to put my thoughts onto paper and write a book that would hopefully clarify some of the misconceptions surrounding the interpretation and application of the Act. Whether I have been is successful is for my audience to judge.

Deciding where to start was the difficult part so I reflected on the problems that I experienced when first exposed to party wall matters in 1997. It was axiomatic that I and many thousands of other surveyors would have to acquire an in-depth knowledge and understanding of the Act to be able to provide the appropriate professional advice to any potential appointing owner(s). Obtaining the professional knowledge proved extremely difficult and frustrating because (i) the Act was in its infancy, and (ii) the subject was shrouded in mystery closely guarded by those surveyor(s) who viewed this niche service as their personal domain. So much so that they would meet for private luncheons and debate the intricacies of interpreting and applying the Act whilst keeping their secrets and practices within their inner-circle. I found this rather bizarre because I believe that we do not own knowledge but are simply custodians with a moral obligation to pass it on to our contemporaries and future generations to debate, develop, and improve. Knowledge has no value or benefit unless we share it.

Accordingly and unfortunately, getting to grips with the Act was very much a matter of *'learning on the job'* with the odd supplemental guidance from those *"august"* but secretive party wall surveyors whose experience was obtained under the earlier legislation. Occasionally those of us lower down the food chain would receive titbits of self-proclaimed wisdom and knowledge from *"they who must be obeyed"* generally in the context of a very rude and aggressive letter advising that *"this is the way we do it and therefore **YOU** should continue to do it this way"*. Those of you that know me will appreciate that I am a pretty laid back guy and most things will go over my head, but one thing that really upsets me are bully's. I will always remember the wise and profound advice that my late father Maurice said to me when I left for my first day at grammar school *"never be a bully and never be bullied"*. I will always listen to polite and reasoned debate and remain open to persuasion. It was Voltaire who said *"I may not agree with what you say, but I will fight to my death your right to say it"* providing you say it politely I will listen. Accordingly, just because something has been done in a certain way for many years does not in my opinion mean it is necessarily correct or that I should accept it. It is interesting to note that some of the more infamous and notorious court cases demonstrate how wrong some of these self-proclaimed and elusive experts interpretations and antiquated practices actually were.

The party wall act created exciting new opportunities for the surveying profession with an overnight explosion of surveyor(s) who immediately promoted themselves within the market place as leading experts on this specialist topic. I soon realised that in reality they were anything but experts. They were simply giving their opinion on legislation that was so new and/or complex that it had not been tested in law and they could not have possibly established a thorough understanding within such a short period of time. Indeed after fifteen years I am still encountering new issues that require careful consideration. I justify this statement by reference to the numbers of cases that are now filtering through the legal system because of the disparity flowing from these practices and interpretations.

My education in party wall matters was further complicated by the fact that the Act has been written in such a way that it is ambiguous and open to misinterpretation. You only have to scratch the surface to recognise that the Act is lacking in detail and qualification on many points. This opinion is shared by others *"ambiguities within the Act make it notoriously difficult to interpret" and "some of these ambiguities predate the introduction of the current Act"*[1] It is therefore understandable that the Act invites conflicting interpretations which creates confusion and disputes amongst the surveyor(s). This is frustrating given that the Act has substantial powers to legalise what were previously illegal activities such as trespass and nuisance. *"The purpose of the Act is to facilitate certain categories of construction operations in the vicinity of property boundaries; consequently it is an enabling Act which in some situations the Act supplants traditional legal concepts. A failure to correctly interpret the Act, its limitations and jurisdiction could lead to a dispute and legal remedies outside of the Act".*[2] In the absence of clarity it is easy to understand why disputes are increasing and why the surveyor(s) are failing to resolve the disputes.

Having now personally been involved in excess of 900 actual party wall awards this observation has continually been reinforced over the years and whilst listening to the opinions and the oral jousting amongst these

---

[1]   Chynoweth, P. *Making Sense of the Party Wall Legislation: Still No Easy Task* Structural Survey Volume 20 No. 1 2002 Page 13.

[2]   Chynoweth, P. (2000) *Invalid Party Wall Awards and How to Avoid Them* Structural Survey Volume 18 No. 4, Page 168.

self-proclaimed experts, I became aware of two distinctly differing approaches and opinions. I believe that the party wall surveying community can be separated into two *'schools'* of interpretation. The first I refer to as the *"old school"*[3] which consists of those surveyor(s) influenced by their historic professional knowledge, practices, and interpretations developed under the earlier Acts. The second are the *"new school"*[4] which consists of those like myself who have studied the legislation from first principles and by applying the natural and ordinary meaning of the English language reach what I consider to be reasoned and practical approaches to applying the principles of the Act.

So having now satisfied myself that my concerns and frustrations are shared, my desire to write this book is not entirely for selfish or egotistical reasons. I am writing this book for the student, old, and new party wall surveyor and anyone with an interest in party wall matters. The intention is to explain the principles of the Act, as I interpret them supported with reference to case law and real life practical examples. I have included personal experiences in support of my opinions where I believe my approach has been correct. If my book promotes healthy debate amongst the new, old, experienced, and inexperienced surveyor(s) and generates why, what, and how questions which subsequently clarify any misunderstandings or confusion then my endeavours will not have been in vain.

1.2 An Overview

Party wall matters are not a new concept to the surveying, legal, and construction profession; indeed, the context of party wall legislation

---

[3]   Pre 1996 Act

[4]   Post 1996 Act

has existed since 1724.[5] The earlier legislation having evolved through successive Act's with one significant difference between the 1996 Act and its more recent predecessors *The London Building (Amendments) Act 1939* & The Bristol Improvement Act 1847. The Act's geographical jurisdiction now extends to the whole of England and Wales, whereas the earlier legislation was restricted to greater London and the Bristol areas. Accordingly, the introduction of the Act had a profound effect on property owner(s) living throughout Britain and Wales *"The impact of this national legislation did not go un-noticed, this had the effect of turning the regime that had operated in London for so long, into a country-wide regime (HHJ Thornton QC: 2010)"*. This created an overnight demand for experienced party wall surveyor(s) which simply did not exist. Without the existence of an award certain aspects of the proposed building works cannot commence so professionals from various backgrounds armed with a copy of the Act, little and/or no understanding of the complexities of the statutory regime, started to provide ancillary services as a *"party wall surveyor"* and so the process began.

The Act creates a statutory regime that enables property owner(s) to undertake certain works that under previous legislation was impossible without the consent of the Adjoining Owner(s). In essence the Act enables an interference with the proprietary rights of another owner(s) property without out fear of liability providing the principles of the Act are properly adopted. *"The 1996 Act is intended to provide an efficient procedure to enable building works that will affect neighbouring owners to be put in hand promptly and on a fair and reasonable basis"*.[6] Getting the procedures right is therefore fundamental to achieving a valid award that legalises *inter alia* previously illegal activities such as trespass and nuisance whilst simultaneously protecting the Adjoining Owner(s)

---

[5]   Chynoweth, P. (2003) *'The Party Wall Case Book,'* Blackwell Publishing Ltd. P.127-137

[6]   Manu v Euroview Investments Ltd [2008] 1 EGLR 165

property from damage and unnecessary inconvenience. The Act is administered by strange creatures called *"party wall surveyor(s)"*[7] that have evolved from various professional backgrounds but predominantly from within the chartered surveying community. They operate within a quasi-judicial position with statutory powers and will determine the issues with the service of an award.[8] The boundaries that the appointed surveyor(s) can operate within are broad and open to interpretation and will only be lawful if the appointed surveyor(s) have a clear understanding of the Act, its relationship with other statutory legislation and/or principles of common law and operate within its boundaries and jurisdiction. Accordingly, the statutory regime is not open to the Building Owner(s) to carry out works without complying with the requirements of the Act.[9] The Act's boundaries inevitably cross into other areas of law *inter alia* easements[10] which *prima facie* may appear to override legal precedents. This was clearly not the intention of the Act, nor could it have been the intention for established principles[11] under common law to supersede the Act, when the Act has an expressed authority to deal with such matters.

The title can be somewhat confusing to the layperson as with many statutes, *"the devil is in the detail"* and the inclusion of *"etc"* is important because the Act is not restricted to the strict definition of the traditional concept of a vertical party structure/wall that separates different owner(s) properties. A floor separating dwellings of different ownership is also classified as a party structure, as are internal elements of a building that separate common areas and occupied parts of buildings. The Act

---

[7]   From many professional disciplines

[8]   Similar to an arbitrators award

[9]   Standard Bank of British and South America v Stokes (1878) L.R 9 Ch.D

[10]   Chapter 11

[11]   Such as easements, trespass, and nuisance

recognises the proprietary rights of Adjoining Owner(s) positioned either above or below the Building Owner(s) property. The surveyor(s) also have jurisdiction to deal with *inter alia* non-contentious[12] issues such as legal costs under various sections of the Act.[13] It must therefore naturally follow that a marriage with other statutory legislation has to be anticipated and accommodated, if the Act is to be successfully and lawfully implemented.

The obligation to serve notice prior to commencement of works rests with the Owner/Occupier(s) desirous of executing certain works[14] and may not necessarily be the freehold title owner(s). Any works executed without an award are unlawful and failure to serve notice can have disastrous consequences when damage occurs. The Act does not provide protection in such circumstances and the courts will not look favourably upon the failure to comply with the statutory provisions of the Act.[15] The exposure to damages and special damages has been reinforced by the courts in a recent case, awarding substantial damages against the offending property owner(s) even where there has been inconclusive evidence of a link between the damages and causation.[16] The duty of care owed by the Building Owner(s) should not be taken lightly.

1.3 Vocabulary

The Act adopts a unique language which is explained with limited definitions under section 20, which I have intentionally positioned at

---

[12] Reeves v Blake [2009] EWCA C iv 611
[13] See Chapter 13
[14] The Building Owner(s)
[15] Louis v Sadiq [1997] 1 EGLR 136; (1998) 59 Con LR 127, Jones & Lovegrove v Ruth & Ruth [2012} EWHC 1538
[16] Jones & Lovegrove v Ruth & Ruth [2012} EWHC 1538 and in the Court of Appeal [2011]

the beginning of this book to allow those new and old to familiarise themselves with these peculiarities before reading about the more complex issues of the Act. The following narrative introduces the various titles of the parties involved in administering the Act and their respective obligations and the process once notice has been served and dissent occurs.

An owner desirous of undertaking building works is referred to as the *'the Building Owner'*, the neighbouring owner(s) are referred to as *'the Adjoining Owner(s) and/or occupiers'*. The Building Owner must serve a valid notice[17] upon the Adjoining Owner(s) before starting the work and invoking the Act. Upon receipt of a notice, the Adjoining Owner(s) can (i) consent to the works, in which case that is an end to the procedures, unless damage arises[18] or alternatively (ii) they may dissent and by agreement appoint a single surveyor[19] referred to as *the 'Agreed Surveyor' or (iii)* in the alternative, each owner can appoint their own surveyor referred to as 'the Building Owners Surveyor' or the 'Adjoining Owners Surveyor' respectively. When two surveyors are appointed they are required to forthwith select[20] another surveyor referred to as 'The Third Surveyor' completing the assembly of the tribunal. The surveyor(s) must settle the matters with the service of a party wall award[21] which will describe the obligations and rights of the respective owner(s). The Third Surveyor will have no active role in the party wall procedures unless either of the owner(s) or the surveyor(s) refers any matter to the Third Surveyor.[22]

---

[17]   Chapter 3, 4 and 8

[18]   Onigbanjo, A. v Mr & Mrs Pearson [2008] The Mayors and City of London Court

[19]   Chapter 12 *para* 12.2

[20]   Note the introduction of *"select"* replaces *appointment*.

[21]   Chapter 12 *para* 12.12

[22]   Chapter 12 *para* 12.3

1.4 Agreements (Outside the Act)

Whilst the legislation is a Statutory instrument, the property owner(s) are of course at liberty to agree (if they wish) to set aside the statutory framework or adopt it at any time. Personally, I do not promote this approach because (i) even though the Act has some inherent defects I see no reason to "re-invent the wheel" and (ii) in any event the issues[23] that would have to be included within the agreement certainly already exist within the Act. However, ultimately it is a matter for the owner(s) to decide. Dr Paul Chynoweth[24] has written a very informative paper on the various types of agreements which are available. Below are my paraphrased explanations of various types of agreement.

1.4.1 Agreements in lieu of Notice

Commonly described as "informal agreements" they purport to contract out of the Act entirely by recording the basis on which it is agreed the works will proceed. These should be recorded by an independent professional (possibly a surveyor or a lawyer) signed and witnessed by the participating owner(s). The parties are at liberty (by agreement) to include anything they wish and is particularly helpful to those parties involved in minor works, where the cost of adopting the provisions of the Act may be substantially greater than the actual cost of executing the works. The parties will be held by the agreement to the extent of those items covered within the agreement. If it transpires that further issues arise after the start of the works, then other agreements will have to be agreed and/or the owners are entitled to rely upon the Act where applicable to resolve these additional issues.

---

[23]   Costs, dispute resolution, extent of the works, access, etc.

[24]   Chynoweth, P. *The Scope for Agreement in Statutory Party Wall Procedures* (2004) 20 Const. L.J. No. 6 © Sweet & Maxwell Limited and contributors.

1.4.2   Agreements subsequent to Notice

The fact that the Building Owner(s) have to serve notice on the Adjoining Owner(s) will not necessarily generate dissent; the Adjoining Owner(s) have the right to consent to the works. In these situations, the provisions of the Act are not set aside[25] the statutory code is simply dormant until it is required to resolve a dispute. If the execution of the works subsequently causes damage, the parties can invoke section 10 to resolve the issues on the basis it was expected that the works would be carried out with the appropriate duty of care and skill without causing damage. The Adjoining Owner(s) did not consent to defective works or to damage and therefore can reasonably rely on section 10.

1.4.3   Agreements to regularise unlawful works

It may be the case that the Building Owner(s) were genuinely unaware of their obligation to serve notice before works commenced. In such circumstances the Building Owner(s) should stop works and regularise matters by instructing their surveyor to prepare the appropriate notices and deal with matters in accordance with the procedures of the Act. In such circumstances the surveyor(s) can only award on outstanding matters. This approach should not be used to produce retrospective awards or deal with damage that occurred prior to the service of the notice unless there is an expressed agreement between the owners.

1.4.4   Agreements relating to variations

This agreement may follow from any one of the three previous types of agreement *supra*, unfortunately construction is not an exact science, where works to an existing building relies on assumptions being made

---

[25]   Onigbanjo, A. v Mr & Mrs Pearson [2008] The Mayors and City of London Court

in respect of the suitability of certain elements of the structure or soil conditions etc, it may not be possible to fully assess the issues until the works commence and further information becomes available or issues arise and the parties reconsider their position and then vary whatever agreements they have previously entered into.

1.5   Jurisdiction

The Act places a statutory duty on the Building Owner(s) to serve notice for works on (i) on the line of junction,[26] (ii) to the party structure, and (iii) for excavations which extend below the foundations of the neighbouring owners structure that are within 3m or 6m[27] of the proposed works. The Acts' statutory powers and the surveyor(s) jurisdiction can only flow from the service of a valid notice and thereafter with an appointment in writing.[28] Upon receipt of a notice the Adjoining Owner(s) have certain obligations and rights which are set out under section 4 & 5.

The Adjoining Owner(s) first obligation is to decide whether to consent or dissent to the notices. The Act anticipates dissent (not dispute) and provides a structured framework which allows and indeed requires the owner(s) to appoint a surveyor(s) to administer the Act. The surveyor(s) role is to resolve the parties respective issues under the Act. *"They are intended to constitute a means of dispute resolution which avoids recourse to the courts".*[29] Further *"The surveyors act in a quasi-judicial position with statutory powers and responsibilities and are required to protect the Adjoining Owners, whose property rights are being*

---

26   Boundary
27   See Figures 17 and 18 and Chapter 8 *para* 8.2 and 8.3
28   Chapter 12 *para* 12.2
29   Reeves v Blake [2009] EWCA C iv 611

compulsorily affected by the application of the Act".[30] In some of the leading cases the party wall surveyor(s) have been referred to as an Arbitrator; *"is that he changes in his capacity from being simply an agent to a quasi-arbitrator.*[31] The use of this title is rather unusual given that the Act does not include any reference to the Arbitration Act or the role of the Arbitrator. *The determination which the surveyor(s) are required to make is more in the nature of an expert determination rather than an arbitrator's award.*[32] When consent is given, the statutory procedures stop subject to the proviso that if damage is caused after the works start, the procedures under section 10 shall apply.[33]

If dissent occurs, section 10 must be applied. *"The steps laid down by the Act should be scrupulously followed throughout and short cuts are not desirable".*[34] There are many examples of where the courts have determined that jurisdiction has not been established because the procedures of the Act have been ignored or incorrectly adopted, and everything done by the surveyor(s) was deemed invalid and a nullity.[35] It never ceases to amaze me how many surveyor(s) get even the most basic steps wrong such as failing to obtain an appointment in writing under section 10(2).

---

[30] Gyle-Thompson v Wall Street (Properties) Ltd 1 WLR 123 [1974] 1 ALL ER 295

[31] Chynoweth, P. (2003) *'The Party Wall Case Book,'* Blackwell Publishing Ltd. P. 253

[32] Chartered Society of Physiotherapy v Simmons Church Smiles [1995] 1 EGLR 88

[33] Onigbanjo, A. v Mr & Mrs Pearson [2008] The Mayors and City of London Court

[34] Gyle-Thompson v Wall Street (Properties) Ltd 1 WLR 123 [1974] 1 ALL ER 295

[35] Gyle-Thompson v Wall Street (Properties) Ltd 1 WLR 123 [1974] 1 ALL ER 295

The Gyle-Thompson case is a clear example of what can go wrong when the surveyor(s) do not understand, or misinterpret the Acts procedures. This case albeit whilst under the earlier 1939 legislation demonstrates the courts approach to ensuring that the surveyor(s) have *"to get it right"*. There are more recent cases which reinforce the courts position. *"Notices should be construed benevolently .... with regards to the fact that it is an instrument intending to take affect between practical men for a practical purpose"* [36] and *"Notices should be .... sufficiently clear and intelligible to enable the Adjoining Owner to decide what action to take"*[37] *"The procedural requirements of the Act and the approach of surveyors to those requirements ought not to be casual. It would be a wise precaution for the surveyor of the Building Owner and the surveyor of the Adjoining Owner to inspect each other's written appointment before they perform their statutory function"*.[38]

1.6   Irregularities and Estoppel

Whilst the Acts procedures are mandatory there may be instances where irregularities are waived either intentionally or by the actions of the owner(s) and or surveyor(s) and the right of estoppel can no longer be relied upon as a defence. *"In my judgement, therefore, a party wall surveyor can by his acts or conduct in the appropriate circumstances waive a defect in a notice or create an estoppel that would bind his appointing owner by accepting to act as though the notice was valid"*.[39] The Adjoining Owner(s) cannot keep what they consider to be an *"ace"* or *"get out of jail"* card up their sleeve, so that if at a later date something goes against them for whatever reason, they can then rely

---

[36]   Manu v Euroview Investments Ltd [2008] 1 EGLR 165
[37]   Hobbs, Hart & Co v Grover [1899] No. 1 Ch 11
[38]   Gyle-Thompson v Wall Street (Properties) Ltd 1 WLR 123 [1974] 1 ALL ER 295
[39]   Manu v Euroview Investments Ltd [2008] 1 EGLR 165

on the irregularity as a quick fix answer to avoid any responsibilities arising out of the application of the Act. *"It seems to me it is far too late now argue that they can set aside the notice, because the whole process is invalid. That cannot be done. You cannot blow hot and cold. Where a party is willing to overlook deficiencies in the other party's application and it is to that other parties advantage that they do so, that other party cannot then say when the going gets a bit rough, well, that is alright, it is not valid. All the assumptions that they have been working under do not apply. That cannot be right and the party is asserting that would be stopped from saying that the notice is of no effect whatsoever".*[40] Providing the surveyor(s) have been properly appointed, their actions can prevent the owner(s) from any future argument in respect on non-compliance with the Act on a legal technicality.

1.7 Technology

Technology has had a major impact on society and has now reached the party wall community. One of the most frustrating things about administering the Act is the copious amounts of paper work that is generated even where there is only one Adjoining Owner. Organising and managing the whole process is extremely difficult and time consuming and time is money, get one element wrong and the whole process starts de novo. This will not only be embarrassing for the surveyor(s) but also expensive especially if the works are delayed while the procedures are regularised. When there are more than one Adjoining Owner/Occupier the whole process becomes even more complicated. I have been involved in party wall matters where there were 32 Adjoining Owner(s) for works under section 1, 2 and 6. This required 224 initial notices, acknowledgement notices, and letters just to inform the parties of the intention to undertake the works. By the time the project had

---

[40]   Sunsaid Property Company Ltd v Omenaka and Omenaka

finished the project had generated in excess of 600 separate documents, all of which have to be managed, retained referenced etc.

The author has developed a software programme (Party Wall Solutions Ltd) *www.partywalls.com* which will generate, file, and collate the documentation at the push of a button making the whole process easier and importantly eliminating the possibility of human error, delays and additional costs. The purchase of this book will entitle the reader to a 1 month no obligation use of the software, send proof of purchase to francesca@partywallsolutions.net and she will contact you and set up your FREE trial period.

1.8   Policing the Act

Given the significance of the Act it is strange that there is no legislative mechanism to force the Building Owner(s) to serve notice and comply with the Act. If they fail to adopt the procedures any works they undertake are unlawful. In such circumstances it is the Adjoining Owner(s) responsibility to ensure the Act is applied and have several options (i) obtain an injunction to stop the unlawful works until the appropriate party wall procedures have been commenced, (ii) alternatively approach the Building Owner(s)[41] and request that they stop works until notice has been served or (iii) do no nothing until damage arises and then initiate legal proceedings. At the very least the Adjoining Owner(s) should write to the Building Owner(s) and record that the works have been started without notice and are unlawful.

---

[41]   Chapter 1 *para* 1.4.3

1.9 Summary

This introduction is intended to provide the reader with a short but effective overview and explanation of the Act, the various parties duties in relation to complying with the statutory regime, and what should be done in the absence of notice. I have endeavoured to explain that the Act, whilst a statutory requirement can be set aside by agreement and having read this chapter the reader should now be able to understand the unique language adopted by the Act.

The complexities of the Act will only be appreciated by the practising party wall surveyor(s) when they encounter a situation that requires clear analytical thought about the Act, its strict wording, and the natural meaning of those words. Accordingly, initiating, interpreting, and applying the Act should not be taken lightly by any party and read as a single document rather than simply relying upon one particular section of the Act. The relationship and inter-dependency between the various sections is clearly demonstrated within this book and it would be an unwise, if not foolish surveyor, who simply looks at the Act whilst wearing blinkers. The consequences of the surveyor(s) getting it wrong can be dire for all concerned not least those Appointing Owner(s) who may be exposed to costs, delays and emotional distress.

Chapter 2　Definitions

2.1　Introduction

The purpose of starting with section 20 is deliberate and intended to introduce those new to the Act to the limited definitions and the unique language used by the Act. In addition it is never a bad thing for those experienced party wall surveyor(s) to reacquaint themselves with the Act's peculiarities. When I first became involved in the Act, I naively believed that it was a clear and unambiguous piece of legislation. I very quickly realised that I was wrong. This is a complex piece of legislation that requires a great deal of thought and consideration when administering the Act. It is essential when considering and interpreting the Act that the full breadth of the Act and its relationship between the various sections and other legislation[42] is considered and understood.

---

[42]　Chapter 1 *para* 1.1

2.2 "Adjoining Owner" and "Adjoining Occupier" respectively mean any owner any occupier of land, buildings, storeys or rooms adjoining those of the Building Owner and for the purposes only of section 6 within the distances specified in that section;

EXPLANATION

The Act does not differentiate between the proprietary rights of the Adjoining Owner(s) and/or the Adjoining Occupier(s). The inclusion of the word "any" also illustrates that there may be more than one person involved with the property. It is not unusual to find that the Adjoining Owner(s) have sub-let the property creating multiple Adjoining Owner(s)/occupier(s). The most critical stage of implementing the Act is to properly identify the Adjoining Owner(s) and/or Occupier(s) legal status and relationship with the property to ensure that the correct owner(s) and occupier(s) to receive notice.

2.3 "building owner means an owner of land who is desirous of exercising rights under this Act;

EXPLANATION

Although the Act refers to a Building Owner (in the singular) it applies in the plural. All of the Building Owner(s) details must be included on all of the notices, and play an active role in the preparation and service of the notice(s) or procedures. This is because there are certain liabilities and obligations arising from the procedures of the Act such as properly appointing the surveyor(s) and to pay the Adjoining Owner(s) reasonable costs[43] or compensation.[44] If the property has more than one

---

[43]   Chapter 12 *para* 12.1.5
[44]   Chapter 9

owner, and one owner acts independently, then anything that they do will be deemed invalid, because one owner cannot stand in the shoes of another. This was illustrated[45] when Mr & Mrs Lehmann received a notice from Mr Herman, they contested the validity of the notice on the grounds that Mrs Hermann had not been included within the notices. Mr & Mrs Lehmann requested that Mrs Herman should undertake to treat herself as bound by the notices in order to regularise the situation. Mrs Herman no doubt persuaded by her husband refused arguing that it was not necessary citing legal precedent[46] and because Mr Herman was the person desirous of undertaking the works and that Mrs Herman would do nothing other than make a *"cup a tea"* for the builders.

The Court drew a distinction between the two cases concluding that the situation in the Crosby v Alhambra case was substantially different to the Lehmann v Herman case. The former relating to receipt of notices by one of two joint tenants, that were held as an effective service of a notice, whilst the service of a notice by one of two building owner(s) on two joint tenants was not. The Court held[47] *"simply in practical terms it would be very odd if the statute provided for one of the two joints owners to deal with an Adjoining Owner without the other joint owner being involved. In real property law terms the concept of one joint owner being able to deal with the property without the other being a party to the transaction has been foreign to English law since the 1925 property legislation. It is therefore important that all building owners are properly identified within the notices."*[48] Taking the extra time to check all of the correct information is included on all notices will avoid a challenge on the validity of the notice(s).

---

45   Lehmann v Herman [1993] 1 EGLR 172
46   Crosby v Alhambra Co Ltd [1907] 1 Ch 295
47   Lehmann v Herman [1993] 1 EGLR 172
48   Chynoweth, P. (2003) *'The Party Wall Case Book,'* Blackwell Publishing Ltd P.22

2.4 "owner" includes—

(a) a person in receipt of, or entitled to receive, the whole or part of the rents or profits of land;

(b) a person in possession of land, otherwise than as a mortgagee or as a tenant from year to year or for a lesser term or as a tenant at will;

(c) a purchaser of an interest in land under a contract for purchase or under an agreement for a lease, otherwise than under an agreement for a tenancy from year to year for a lesser term;

EXPLANATION

It is not unusual to have a number of leases and sub-leases within a single building and as this definition suggests they may all be owner(s) and entitled to notice. For the purposes of serving notice I recommend that where there is doubt, the surveyor should exercise caution and treat them all as individual owner(s). Whilst the intention to prevent delays and mistakes from arising is commendable, there may be some who would criticise this approach, I would suggest that it is a pragmatic and sensible approach because the minimal costs in serving notice (which can be withdrawn) can far out way any losses incurred if matters are delayed because a person suddenly claims that they are an owner and are entitled to notice. However, this approach does incur potential abortive costs so I would recommend obtaining the Building Owner(s) agreement prior adopting this strategy.

The Act helpfully introduces three categories of an *"owner"* whilst also recognising the legal title of a person(s) purchasing a property under contract.[49] Where contracts have been exchanged for the purchase and/

---

[49]   Spiers and Son Ltd v Troup (1915) 84 LJKB 1986

or lease with completion to follow, the purchaser(s) tenants are now defined under the Act as an owner because they have *prima facie* a legal interest in the property. Accordingly, they are entitled to serve and/or receive notice for any intended works. This situation arises more commonly in commercial situations where a developer wants to start their development as soon as possible after completion of the purchase and will therefore commence the statutory procedures as soon as possible after signing the contracts.

This approach is not without pitfalls and the importance of getting it right is demonstrated in Spiers & Son v Troup. Spiers & Son were contractors engaged by the Building Owner(s) to develop an investment property on behalf of Troup and also began negotiations to agree a 99 year lease on one of the properties under development. In anticipation of reaching an agreement Spiers & Son served a notice for works to the party wall as "the Building Owner". However it was held that because the negotiations of the lease had not been concluded, they did not have a legal interest in the property and therefore were not the Building Owner(s). The notice was deemed invalid[50] because it is not until an exchange of contracts occurs that the purchaser has a legal interest in the property and thereafter the vendor and purchaser are joint owners. On completion of the contract the ownership reverts to the new purchaser. Unfortunately, the Act and indeed the law is silent on the correct procedures if completion occurs before an award is made or whilst the works are on-going. It is not clear whether the vendor's obligations would cease on completion of the sale when they are recorded within the award as an owner. What would happen if the purchaser caused damage to an Adjoining Owner(s) that they were unable to financially repair, would the vendor have an on-going obligation under the award to make good this loss or damage?

---

[50]   Spiers and Son Ltd v Troup (1915) 84 LJKB 1986

2.5 "foundation", in relation to a wall, means the solid ground or artificially formed support resting on solid ground on which the wall rests;

EXPLANATION

This is the first of two types of foundation referred to under the Act and relate to excavations[51] to a predetermined depth and width, filled with concrete or some other approved material for the purpose of supporting the structure built thereon or adjacent to[52] and designed to safely distribute any loads on to the solid ground on which it rests. The Building Owner(s) have the right[53] to project the foundation for any wall subject to notice under the Act onto the Adjoining Owner(s) property without their consent. The use of the word "project" is a clear statement that only the part of the foundation that is not directly below the wall can be placed on the Adjoining Owner(s) land.[54] Because excavations can have an impact on the natural right of support[55] enjoyed by Adjoining Owner(s) they are entitled to be informed of these works. The projecting foundations (figure 1) are not allowable because the wall is not on the line of junction, whereas the projecting foundation in figure 4 is allowable without consent because the wall is on the line of junction.

---

[51]   Chapter 8
[52]   Natural right of support
[53]   Chapter 3 *para* 3.6
[54]   Chapter 8 *para* 8.2 and 8.3
[55]   Chapter 11 *para* 11.5

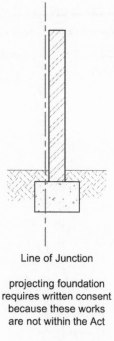

Line of Junction

projecting foundation
requires written consent
because these works
are not within the Act

figure 1

2.6 "special foundations" means foundations in which an assemblage of beams or rods is employed for the purpose of distributing any load; and

EXPLANATION

This second definition introduces one simple but important distinction between the two types of foundations which is the inclusion of reinforcement which increases the structural integrity of the foundations ability to distribute any load imposed thereon. The Act does not specify what quantity or level of reinforcement is necessary to qualify them as a special foundation, so in the absence of any minimum requirement I would suggest that any use of reinforcement or mesh must create a special foundation.[56] The right to project foundations onto the Adjoining Owner(s) is removed when special foundations are adopted unless written consent is obtained[57] and the proposed wall being subject to notice under the Act.

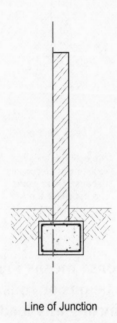

Line of Junction

requires written consent
under Section 7(4) for
special foundations and
Notice under Section 1(5)

figure 2

2.7 **"party fence wall" means a wall (not being part of a building) which stands on lands of different owners and is used or constructed to be used for separating such adjoining lands, but does not include a wall constructed on the land of one owner the artificially formed support of which projects into the land of another owner;**

EXPLANATION

A wall that is not part of a building and is astride the boundary or line of junction of two properties irrespective of the position of the boundary within the wall (see figure 3 & 4) is a party fence wall and subject to notice under the Act. A wall away from the boundary (see figure 5) and on the land of one owner is not subject to notice.

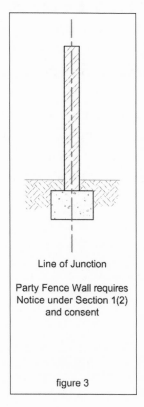

Line of Junction

Party Fence Wall requires Notice under Section 1(2) and consent

figure 3

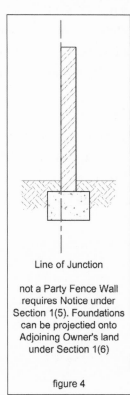

Line of Junction

not a Party Fence Wall requires Notice under Section 1(5). Foundations can be projectied onto Adjoining Owner's land under Section 1(6)

figure 4

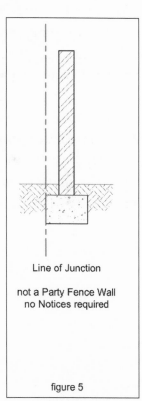

Line of Junction

not a Party Fence Wall no Notices required

figure 5

2.8 "party structure" means a party wall and also a floor partition or other structure separating buildings or parts of buildings approached solely by separate staircases or separate entrances;

EXPLANATION

A party structure applies to both the vertical and horizontal elements of a building, which separates properties that are in different ownership. This will also include *inter alia* walls and floors that separate properties (figure 6) or common areas, stairwells, and landings. Establishing which elements of a building are a party wall can be extremely difficult.[58] Accordingly, the surveyor(s) should have an understanding of construction technology and insofar as it is reasonable to do so, advise the Building Owner(s) when they should serve notice. For example a plasterboard ceiling, insulation, floor joists and floor boarding are all part of the floor structure, a laminate wood flooring if overlaid on to the structural floor is not part of the structure. If used as an alternative to floor boards or chipboard flooring, then it will form part of the structural floor and uplifting or replacing requires notice. Furthermore, a suspended ceiling below a party structure (floor) for decorative purposes is not part of the party structure unless it contributes towards the fire resistance and sound proofing qualities[59] at which time it becomes an intrinsic element of the structure and requires notice.

---

58 Flying freehold
59 Building Regulation Requirement

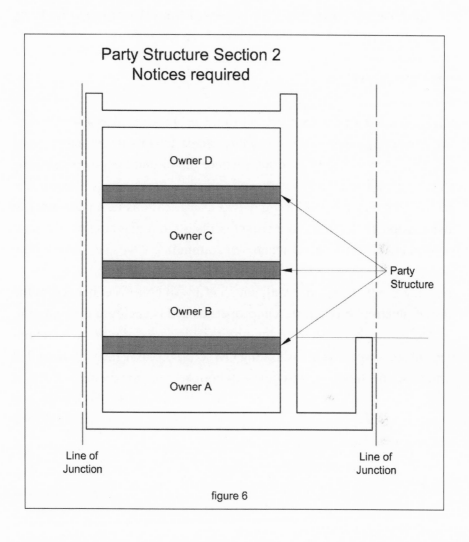

Party Structure Section 2
Notices required

Owner D

Owner C

Owner B

Owner A

Party Structure

Line of Junction

Line of Junction

figure 6

2.9 "party wall" means—

(a) **a wall which forms part of a building and stands on lands of different owners to a greater extent than the projection of any artificially formed support on which the wall rests; and**

EXPLANATION

Before 1926 the primary meaning of a *"party wall"* was a wall which two Owner(s) shared and were *prima facie* tenants in common.[60] The same conclusion might be drawn where the circumstances of how the wall was built are unknown[61] and helpfully, the Act now considers such circumstances and provides two classifications of a party wall to avoid disputes. In addition a recent decision in a planning appeal case reinforces this principle of tenants in common.[62]

The first is a type (a) party wall which is a wall built (i) either across the line of junction of two different properties and is enclosed upon for any part of its height or width or length or (ii) is across the line of junction and enclosed upon by an Adjoining Owner(s) building (see figures 7-11) which demonstrates the principles in both section and plan.

---

[60]   Watson v Gray (1880) 14 Ch.D 192 at 194

[61]   Cubit v Porter (1828) 8 B. & C. 257

[62]   Chapter 9 *para* 9.6.1

shaded sections of
wall is
Type (A) Party Wall

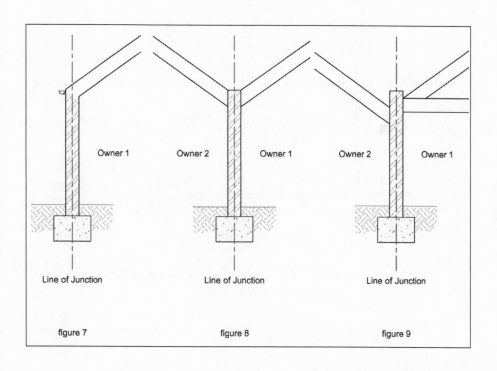

figure 7 figure 8 figure 9

plan views of
Type (A) Party Wall

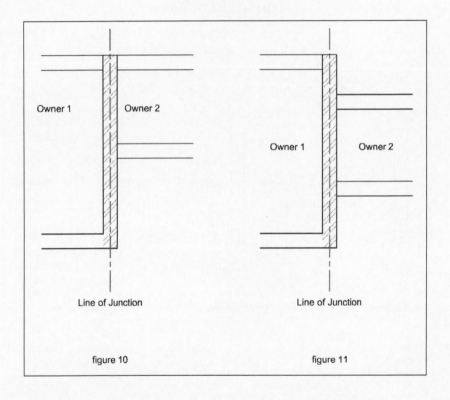

Owner 1 · Owner 2

Line of Junction

figure 10

Owner 1 · Owner 2

Line of Junction

figure 11

It is not unusual for owner(s) to be in dispute about the position of the line of junction which is for the avoidance of doubt a matter of legal title. Unfortunately, there will be occasions where the surveyor(s) may have to establish the position of the line of junction to determine the status of the wall. The issue of whether appointed surveyor(s) can make a determination on a point of law has been decided in recent case law[63] where the Third Surveyor had determined the position of the line of junction to bring the dispute to its natural conclusion, the award was appealed on the principle that only the courts could determine a point of law.

It was held by HHJ Cowell that *"It seems to me that an arbitrator, a third surveyor does have jurisdiction to decide a matter, even if it is a matter of law, which is fundamental to the question of whether he makes an award or not. It is possible for an arbitrator to say "this is a matter of law, it ought to be decided by a court first, then bring it back to me:", but I can see nothing wrong with the arbitrator saying: "I must decide this point because it is fundamental. I will decide it and I will say what my award will be on one basis or another."*

The position of the line of junction is a critical element in determining whether the wall is or is not a party wall, *"It would be a very strange situation, if an issue on a point of law prevented the surveyors from reaching a natural conclusion. Where the quantity of land that each owner has contributed to the site of the wall is known, the property in the wall follows the property in the land"*.[64] The appointed surveyor(s) duty is to bring the procedures to a natural conclusion with an award.[65] The procedures adopted by the surveyor(s) when determining the position of the line of junction should be fully recorded within the award. A

---

[63] Loost v Kremer [1997] West London County Court 12 May (Unreported)

[64] Matts v Hawkins (1813) 5 Taunt 20

[65] Chapter 12 *para* 12.12

failure to record everything within the award[66] could allow a successful appeal.

"party wall" means—

(b) so much of a wall not being a wall referred to in paragraph (a) above as separates buildings belonging to different owners;

EXPLANATION

The definition of a type (b) wall was determined in an early case where *"the words party wall are used, not in their technical sense, but as a convenient phrase for dividing wall ... The walls in question here will be dividing walls up to the top of the first storey, and to that extent section 75 applies to them, any point above cease to be a party wall where not enclosed upon"* [67] (see figures 12 &13) positioned wholly within the land of one owner but is enclosed upon by the Adjoining Owner(s) structure is a type (b) party wall. It can be enclosed upon for the full height and length or any part thereof but it is only the section within the enclosure that is a party wall. The unenclosed areas are not a party wall[68] (see figure 12, 13 & 14) and the enclosing Owner(s) will have limited legal rights over those remaining sections of the wall.[69] If the enclosing structure is removed, the remaining wall's status changes back to a wall built wholly on the land of one owner. The Adjoining Owner(s) cannot later enclose upon the dominant structure without consent or unless they can demonstrate they have a legal right at common law to do so.

---

66 Davies & Sleep v Wise [2006] Barnet County Court
67 Drury v Army & Navy Auxiliary Cooperative Supply Ltd (1896) 2 QB 271
68 Western v Arnold (1873) 8 Ch A pp 1084.
69 Chapter 11 *para* 11.5

If or when a trespass by enclosure occurs, the dominant owner(s) should immediately request that the encroaching subservient owner(s) remove the trespassing structure. Remaining silent is not an advisable course of action because the encroaching owner(s) can through the passage of time[70] obtain certain property rights under the laws of adverse possession.[71] However, these procedures have in recent years become more difficult since the introduction of The Land Registration Act 2002.

shaded sections of
of wall is a
Type (B) Party Wall

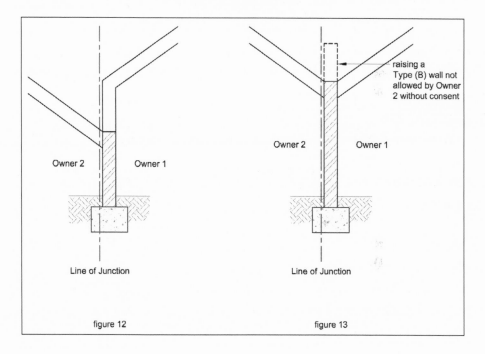

---

[70]   The Prescription Act 1832

[71]   Prudential Assurance Co Ltd v Waterloo Real Estate Inc (1999) 2 EGLR 85

plan view of
Type (B) Party Wall

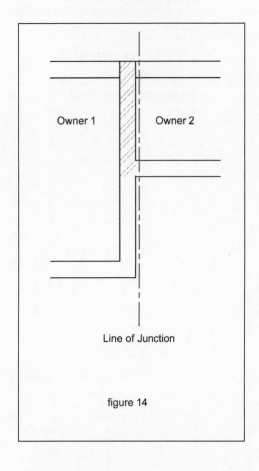

Owner 1

Owner 2

Line of Junction

figure 14

2.10 "surveyor" means any person not being a party to the matter appointed or selected under section 10 to determine disputes in accordance with the procedures set out in this Act.

EXPLANATION

The Act allows the owner(s)[72] or indeed the surveyor(s)[73] to appoint anyone as a surveyor, so as long as they are not *"a party to the matter"* which indicates that a degree of impartiality is envisaged. Unfortunately, *"any person not being a party to the matter"* is not a particularly helpful, definition because the owner(s) may appoint any member of their family which creates a very unique scenario with regards to the principal of perceived or actual *"conflict of interest"*. Just how far this issue can be taken is open to debate, if the procedures of the Act are properly implemented there is nothing the owner(s) or indeed any external organisation can do once the appointments have been made unless they are invalid.[74] It is not uncommon for the Building Owner(s) to appoint his Architect, but is that reasonable given that the appointed surveyor(s) duty is to critically assess the works,[75] would an Architect be as objective and critical of his design as an independent party wall surveyor?

The legality of this dual role has been addressed,[76] *HHJ Cowell: "....* *the mere fact that he has acted as architect does not, in my judgment mean that he must disqualify himself . . . ." . . . . he changes in his*

---

[72]   Chapter 12 *para* 12.2

[73]   Chapter 12 *para* 12.4 and 12.6

[74]   Chapter 12 *para* 12.19

[75]   Design, specification

[76]   Loost v Kremer [1997] West London County Court 12 May (Unreported)

capacity from being simply an agent to a quasi-arbitrator and he has to bear in mind those are his duties . . . . that is all there really is to this point."[77] It would fall upon the Appointed Surveyor(s) to conduct themselves properly and absent of any wrong doing could not be criticised for making or accepting the appointment or selection[78]. Some institutions adopt a different approach and in my opinion mistakenly and wrongly misinterpret the Act, the surveyor(s) duties and indeed the surveyor(s) own ability to act impartially irrespective of whether there is a pre-existing relationship between the surveyor(s) is for the surveyor(s) to determine and or ultimately the courts.

2.11 "appointing officer" means the person appointed under this Act by the local authority to make such appointments as are required under section 10(8);

EXPLANATION

When dissent has occurred the two surveyors are required[79] to *"forthwith select"* another surveyor referred to as the Third Surveyor. If the two surveyor(s) cannot agree, then either of the surveyor(s) must refer the matter to the local authority appointing officer[80] who is required to make the selection on their behalf, thereafter the appointing officer has no further involvement. If the surveyor(s) proceed absent of a Third Surveyor everything they have done will be *ultra viries*.

---

[77]   Chynoweth, P. (2003) *'The Party Wall Case Book,'* Blackwell Publishing Ltd.

[78]   Third Surveyor

[79]   Chapter 12 *para* 12.2.1

[80]   Chapter 12 *para* 12.10

2.12 Supplemental Definitions

Unfortunately, the Act randomly introduces words to describe various elements of a building and/or obligations without providing in my opinion a clear definition which I believe is a primary cause of confusion and debate amongst surveyors. With the intention of provoking healthy debate, I would hasten to introduce these supplemental definitions based (I would add) on my own experience, interpretation, and approach to party wall matters. Accept or ignore as you wish:

"structure" means the arrangement of and the relationship between the parts or elements of a building or other object constructed and arranged according to a plan.

This definition appears at first blush to be open to all sorts of interpretations, but I do not think that it should, because it must naturally follow that in the context of the Act we are dealing with works that require notice[81] and therefore applying the ordinary and natural meaning of the words I would therefore suggest that pavements, drains, and inspection chambers, concrete bases, electric pylons, garden walls, swimming pools and rockeries or indeed anything that is artificially created will fall within the definition of a structure and therefore be subject to notice.[82]

"on" in relation to determining whether section 1(5) applies, the ordinary and natural meaning of *"on"* must be *"on"* the surface or in contact with a part or an element of an adjoining owner(s) structure that is positioned *"on"* the line of junction under the Act.

---

[81] Chapter 2, 3 and 8

[82] Chapter 8

"partition" means the arrangement of and the relationship between the parts or elements of the structure that separates the whole or parts of buildings under different ownership and or occupation and must by definition be either a type (a) or (b) party wall under the Act.

"footings" means the arrangement of and the structural function of the parts or elements of the substructure below ground level which is intended to support and/or distribute the loads from a structure or other object constructed on or against it according to a design that provides stability.

"compensate" means to make amends for any reasonable loss or injury arising out of the works and /or their execution that are subject to notice and is not limited to putting the affected property owner(s) back into the same position as if the damage or loss had not arisen.

"dispute" means the owner is entitled to resist the actions of another party insofar as they have a right under a specific section of the Act to protect their property and/or quiet enjoyment thereof.

"dissent" means to withhold assent to the proposed works and to adopt the procedures of the Act.

"drilling" means the same as "cutting" into for the purposes of penetrating the ground, structure, and or any of its elements. The depth of penetration for cutting or drilling is irrelevant for the purposes of applying section 2.

"due diligence" means to proceed with the notifiable works in accordance with the reasonable and normal programme of construction activities.

"basement" if the vertical (walls) elements include an assemblage of beams and or rods and/or are linked to the horizontal (floor) elements and are dependent on the bond created between the reinforcement of the designed basement structure they are for the purposes of the Act a special foundation.

2.13 Summary

It is helpful that the Act has included a selection of definitions, unfortunately, in my opinion the Act has not gone far enough to explain the intricate, unique, and random language and principals introduced and used by the Act. The powers that allow the appointed surveyor(s) to interfere with the proprietary rights of property owner(s) which has for centuries been within the domain of common and general law must be non-contentious. If the Act fails to provide clarity on important aspects that are fundamental to its application, it is inevitable that the ambiguity will create conflicting interpretations. Obviously, this was not the intention when the Act was drafted, but having now been in existence for 15 years it is abundantly clear that this is exactly what is happening and on a regular basis. Accordingly, based on my own experience, interpretations, and approach to party wall matters I have introduced additional definitions which are intended to provide further clarity, although I fully anticipate that they may or may not be accepted.

Chapter 3 Section 1—Construction and repair of walls on the line of junction

3.1 Introduction

Few disputes will raise passions as strongly as boundary disputes and establishing the position of the boundary is fundamental to implementing this section of the Act. The inclusion of repairs to an existing wall[83] is also available under other legislation. This section sets out the formal procedures that the Building Owner(s) must adopt if they intend to either construct a new wall on or across the line of junction or to execute repairs to an existing wall. The Act anticipates that these activities will be non-contentious and accordingly the Adjoining Owner(s) cannot object or prevent the works from proceeding subject to ensuring that the Adjoining Owner(s) property and statutory rights are not adversely affected.

3.2 Line of Junction works

1   (1) This section shall have effect where lands of different owners adjoin and—

(a)   are not built on at the line of junction; or

---

[83]   The Access to Neighbouring Land Act 1992

(b)   are built on at the line of junction only to the extent of a boundary wall (not being a party fence wall or to the external wall of a building),

and either owner is about to build on any part of the line of junction.

EXPLANATION

Where there is an intention to construct either a new wall on the line of junction or undertake repairs to an existing wall notice must be given to the Adjoining Owner(s). The Building Owner(s) cannot exercise any of the rights[84] under the Act unless the notice has been served and the procedures adopted. Any works to raise or alter an existing party fence or boundary wall built on the line of junction are excluded. This limitation is particularly frustrating for the Building Owner(s) who may want to adopt an existing party fence wall which is structurally sound but technically and physically impossible to raise or alter without having access to satisfy health and safety legislation and or to avoid committing a trespass by working overhand. Accordingly, the Building Owner(s) will have to reach an agreement[85] with the Adjoining Owner(s). If an agreement cannot be reached the Building Owner(s) can demolish the existing wall and serve notice[86] under section 1(5) for a *"new wall"* to invoke the procedures under the Act.

---

[84]   Chapter 10 *para* 10.2

[85]   Chapter 1 *para* 1.3

[86]   Chapter 2 *para* 2.12 and chapter 3 *para* 3.6

3.3   Service of Notice

s.1(2)

(2)   If a building owner desires to build a party wall or party fence wall on the line of junction he shall, at least one month before he intends the building work to start, serve on any Adjoining Owner a notice which indicates his desire to build and describes the intended wall.

EXPLANATION

The notice must include a description of the wall and be served 1 month before the intended commencement date. The Act recognises that executing these works will involve trespassing onto and interfering with the Adjoining Owner(s) quite enjoyment of their property and seeks to minimise this by including a minimum period of notice before commencing the works. The works cannot proceed even if an award has been prepared and served until the expiry of this notice period.

3.4   Adjoining Owner(s) consent

s.1(3)

(3)   If, having been served with notice described in subsection (2), an Adjoining Owner serves on the building owner a notice indicating his consent to the building of a party wall or party fence wall—

(a)   the wall shall be built half on the land or each of the two owners or in such other position as may be agreed between the two owners; and

(b)   the expense of building the wall shall be from time to time defrayed by the two owners in such proportion as has regard to the use made or to be made of the wall by each of them and to the cost of labour and materials prevailing at the time when that use is made by each owner respectively.

EXPLANATION

The construction of a wall across the line of junction creates significant legal issues and opportunities, requiring the Adjoining Owner(s) consent to regularise what is a trespass. When consent is given the procedures under section 10 do not apply and simply falls away[87]. However, I am constantly amazed by the numbers of Owner(s) who do the strangest things with their largest single asset without realising the legal consequences of what they have consented to or without producing sufficient documentation to record the agreement.[88] Indeed issues may not arise until sometime in the future when either existing or future owner(s) attempt to do something to the wall which creates a fresh dispute. The cost of constructing the wall will initially be paid by the Building Owner(s) but if the Adjoining Owner(s) want to adopt the wall at some time in the future[89] the costs of constructing the wall will have to be addressed.

3.5 Adjoining Owner(s) non-consent

s.1(4)

(4) If, having been served with notice described in subsection (2), an Adjoining Owner does not consent under this subsection to the building of a party wall or party fence wall, the building owner may only build the wall—

---

[87] Onigbanjo, A. v Mr & Mrs Pearson [2008] The Mayors and City of London Court

[88] Chapter 1 *para* 1.3

[89] Chapter 12 *para* 13.3

(a) at his own expense; and

(b) as an external wall or a fence wall, as the case may be, placed wholly on his own land,

and consent under this subsection is consent by a notice served within the period of fourteen days beginning with the day on which the notice described in section (2) is served.

EXPLANATION

The Adjoining Owner(s) can withhold consent without providing any explanation requiring the Building Owner(s) to build the wall on their land. If they require access, the works must be *"in pursuance of the Act"* and *"on"*[90] the line of junction to establish a right of access[91] for the construction of the wall. Although an automatic right of access is available for the excavation and projection of foundations.[92] The cost of these works would fall upon the Building Owner(s).

3.6   On the line of junction

s.1(5)

(5) If the building owner desires to build on the line of junction a wall placed wholly on his own land he shall, at least one month before he intends the building work to start, serve on any adjoining a notice which indicates his desire to build and describes the intended wall.

---

[90]   Chapter 3 *para* 3.5
[91]   Chapter 10 *para* 10.2
[92]   Chapter 2 *para* 2.5

EXPLANATION

Quite simply, if the proposed wall is away from the line of junction for any distance it is not *"on"* the line of junction and section 1 does not apply.[93] Properly interpreting what will satisfy *"on"*[94] is fundamental, if the right to interfere with the proprietary rights of the Adjoining Owner(s) can be lawfully executed. Section 1(1) defines the line of junction as *"where lands of different owners adjoin'* it is not per se the boundary. *"The application of section 1 has given rise to some difficulty, it contains the self-contradictory concept of a wall which is built on the boundary and yet is also placed on the land of one owner"*.[95] This is a principal that some surveyor(s) have struggled with over the years.

The interpretation of section 1 is arguably one of the most debated sections of the Act, one publication[96] includes three interpretations which demonstrates the disparity within that particular organisation and its authors. The confusion surrounding this interpretation is also evident in other publications, *"I would suggest that if the courts were asked to define "on" they would apply one of a number of plain and natural meaning (sic) such as "in contact or connection with", "attached to" or "in the immediate vicinity of" These definitions would sit comfortably*

---

[93]   Davies & Sleep v Wise [2006] Barnet County Court

[94]   Antino, P. *'Using the Party Wall etc. Act 1996 to gain access to a neighbouring property'* Emerald Group Publishing Limited, Structural Survey, Journal of Building Pathology and Refurbishment, Vol. 29 issue No 3 2011 pp. 210-220

[95]   Bickford-Smith, S. and Sydenham, C. 3rd Ed, (2009) *"Party Walls Law and Practice"*, Jordan Publishing Ltd

[96]   The Pyramus & Thisbe Club *"The Party Wall Act explained: 'A Commentary on the Party Wall etc. Act 1996"* The Pyramus & Thisbe Club

within both s.1(2) and 1(5) of the Act without causing confusion or absurdity".[97]

I would agree with Ainsworth's suggestion that *"in contact or connection with"* or *"attached to"* will satisfy the definition[98] of *"on"* but only at the point of contact between the line of junction and/or the structure. I do not accept Ainsworth's suggestion *"in the immediate vicinity of"* can reasonably have the same meaning as *"on"*. The best way to construe a document is to read it as it would have read at the time it was written, accordingly, it could not have been the intention when drafting the Act to adopt such a wide interpretation. In my opinion Ainsworth's suggestion *"in the immediate vicinity of"* is too vague and open to further interpretation and abuse by owner(s) and surveyor(s) alike and most certainly creates an absurdity.

If we accepted Ainsworth's suggestion one could argue that 10mm or 300mm is within the immediate vicinity and therefore should be interpreted as *'on'* the line of junction. I disagree and believe that Ainsworth's suggestion is flawed. In my opinion the Act is explicit, if the wall is away from the line of junction for any distance, it will be wholly within the Building Owner(s) land and cannot by definition be *"on"* the line of junction and therefore is not subject to notification.

A good example of the confusion flowing from the interpretation of section 1(5) is demonstrated in an appeal[99] which turned on whether

---

[97]   Ainsworth, R., *Differences of Opinion Interpreting Section 1*, Structural Survey Vol. 18 No 5 2000 pp. 213-217

[98]   Antino, P. *'Using the Party Wall etc. Act 1996 to gain access to a neighbouring property'* Emerald Group Publishing Limited, Structural Survey, Journal of Building Pathology and Refurbishment, Vol. 29 issue No 3 2011 pp. 210-220

[99]   Davies & Sleep v Wise [2006] Barnet County Court.

the Third Surveyor had properly interpreted the definition of *"on"*. A dispute was referred to the Third Surveyor, who determined that the proposed works satisfied section 1(5) and that the Building Owner(s) were entitled to a right of access.[100] Having served notice[101] the Building Owner(s) mistakenly expected a right of access to build a single storey rear extension that was close to, but not on the line of junction. The Third Surveyors Award was appealed[102] the Adjoining Owner(s) argued that the works were *"not in pursuance of the Act"* and therefore did not satisfy the requirements of section 8(1). Demonstrating compliance with section 1(5) was critical to the Building Owner(s) success. Unfortunately, the Third Surveyor's award was silent on how he had reached his decision.

In her judgment HHJ Pearl records, *'I am referred to the authority of Saul v Norfolk County Council on the statutory interpretation of the words "for the purposes of executing any work in pursuance of this Act". It was held within that case that reference to the words "in pursuance of the said part III, these words cannot in our judgement be otiose, some force must be given to them if they are given their ordinary and natural meaning . . . . the ordinary natural meaning is, in our judgement in exercise of the authority conferred by part IIII", In any event, since the full facts of the case[103] are not known here, it is perhaps a little unwise to speculate as to why certain arguments were or were not put before the learned judge. The important point is that in coming to her decision, HHJ Pearl was limited to the evidence and the arguments that were put before her'.*

---

[100]   Chapter 10 *para* 10.2

[101]   Chapter 3 *para* 3.5 and Chapter 8 *para* 8.2

[102]   Chapter 12 *para* 12.19

[103]   The Building Owner failed to demonstrate that the works satisfied section 8(1).

Continuing: *the Third Surveyor's award confers access for the 'reasonable purpose of carrying out the terms of each notice and a subsequent award'. These are not words which come from the Act, and if they are meant to paraphrase the words in the Act then I find that the words used in the award place an inaccurate gloss on the words of the Act. Further, where words are used in a statute more than once then the interpretation of the words must be consistent throughout. The words 'in pursuance of this Act' also appear in section 7(2) of the Act in connection with compensation. I am satisfied, that if the words meant what that the Third Surveyor says they mean in this case, it would create a capricious situation where an Adjoining Owner could be liable to pay compensation and could accordingly be interpreted to impose the positive burden to compensate when none exists in common law.*

*A surveyor only has jurisdiction to allow access under section 8(1) of the Act "for the purposes of executing **any work in pursuance of the Act**" 'I emphasise I heard no argument that the respondents*[104] *require access to the appellants*[105] *land for any purposes which would fall within any of the limited categories of section 1, 2 or section 6 of the Act'.* The appeal was therefore upheld.

This case clearly establishes that the right to access[106] will turn on whether or not the wall is or is not being built '*on*' the line of junction. Adopting the natural and ordinary meaning of the word '*on*' was the critical point which the Building Owner(s) failed to do. However, this is a County Court judgement and does not set any binding legal precedent, although it is in my opinion persuasive and of value to other courts or parties involved in party wall procedures.

---

[104] The Building Owner(s)
[105] The Adjoining Owner(s)
[106] Chapter 10 *para* 10.2

3.7 Projecting foundations

s.1(6)

(6) Where the building owner builds a wall wholly on his own land in accordance with subsection (4) or (5) he shall have the right, at any time in the period which—

(a) begins one month after the day on which the notice mentioned in the subsection concerned was served, and

(b) ends twelve months after that day,

to place below the level of the land of the Adjoining Owner such projecting footings and foundations as are necessary for the construction of the wall.

EXPLANATION

In my opinion this section of the Act is bizarre to say the least, because it allows a right to trespass onto and excavate *"foundations"*[107] on an Adjoining Owner(s) land, but only if they *"are necessary"*. I cannot think of any situation where it is necessary to position foundations onto another person's land. Whilst there may be practical or financial reasons for doing so, that does not mean that the foundation design is *"necessary"*. Foundations can be designed in a number of ways, for example a traditional mass filled foundation can be increased in width to resist rotational movement so the wall can be built on the external edge of the foundation which can be excavated *"on"* the line of junction thus maintaining a right of access[108] without projecting foundations onto

---

[107] Not special foundations
[108] Chapter 10 *para* 10.2

the Adjoining Owner(s) land which in my opinion makes perfect sense and will avoid any potential future disputes.

Projecting foundations on to another owner(s) property will expose the Building Owner(s) to all sorts of additional costs and potential liabilities for damage, inconvenience, and nuisance.[109] Even if the Building Owner(s) could demonstrate that the projecting foundations were necessary, the Adjoining Owner(s) can at any time cut away the projecting footing[110] or can they? If we consider the restrictions imposed under section 9[111] how can section 1(6) (i) create a right to interfere with the right of support[112] and if so, (ii) are the Adjoining Owner(s) responsible for any additional strengthening works that may be necessary as a consequence of their cutting away the projecting foundations. If we consider that the projecting foundations were positioned without their consent, does this now create an easement by agreement, how it can be reasonable to impose future liabilities on to the Adjoining Owner(s). Clearly, a number of questions arise out of the application of this section and the arguments for and against projecting foundations will be many and varied but the correct and most sensible approach in my opinion is to avoid them like the plague.

3.8   Compensation for projecting foundations

s.1(7)

(7)   Where the building owner builds a wall wholly on his own land in accordance with subsection (4) or (5) he shall do so at his own expense and shall compensate any Adjoining Owner and any adjoining occupier for any damage to his property occasioned by—

---

[109]   Chapter 3 *para* 3.6, and Chapter 9 *para* 9.2

[110]   Chapter 3 *para* 3.6

[111]   Chapter 11

[112]   Chapter 11 *para* 11.5

(a)   the building of the wall;

(b)   the placing of any footings or foundations placed in accordance with subsection (6).

EXPLANATION

This section confirms my concerns raised about the potential risk associated with the projection of foundations onto the Adjoining Owner(s) land and the difficulties that may arise if the Adjoining Owner(s) decide to cut away the projecting foundation. The surveyor(s) have jurisdiction to award costs against the Building Owner(s) and are required to compensate the Adjoining Owner(s) for any damage which is caused and/or is reasonably foreseeable from excavating on their land.

The obligation *"to compensate"*[113] the Adjoining Owner(s) opens a wide area of debate. Let's suppose that at some time in the future the Adjoining Owner(s) decide to undertake certain building works that require the removal of the Building Owner(s) projecting *"foundations"*. Naturally, this will incur costs for the Adjoining Owner(s) that would not have arisen if the Building Owner(s) had not exercised their rights[114] in the first instance. Therefore, are the Adjoining Owner(s) entitled to receive compensation from the Building Owner(s) for these additional costs? In my opinion applying the ordinary and natural meaning of the word compensation[115] they are entitled to reimbursement of these additional costs.

Unfortunately the problem does not finish there, what would happen if the Building Owner(s) sold their property, would the new purchaser be liable to compensate the Adjoining Owner(s). The only opinion that I have found on this point is *"They are in relatively little jeopardy for*

---

[113]   Chapter 3 *para* 3.6

[114]   Chapter 3 *para* 3.7

[115]   Chapter 2 *para* 2.12

the works undertaken. They will in principle be liable for works which they undertake but not already undertaken".[116] If this opinion is correct the Adjoining Owner(s) are now left with the additional costs of cutting away the projecting foundations and possibly providing additional support to the remaining foundation.

I can only reiterate that in my opinion caution should always be exercised when considering whether to project foundations[117] on to the Adjoining Owner(s) land. The surveyor(s) must consider the implications and fully advise the owner(s) of the inherent risks and liabilities.[118] The increased costs of perhaps redesigning a foundation, so that it remains wholly within the Building Owner(s) land could in the long term be significantly cheaper than any potential damages and/or claims arising out of the projecting foundation.

3.9   Disputes under section 1

s.1(8)

(8)   Where any dispute arises under this section between the building owner and any Adjoining Owner or occupier it is to be determined in accordance with section 10.

EXPLANATION

The Adjoining Owner(s) cannot under section 1 dissent to the works because the Building Owner(s) can build whatever they want on their own land. However, a dispute may for example occur if damage arises

---

[116]   Bickford-Smith, S. and Sydenham, C. 3rd Ed, (2009) *"Party Walls Law and Practice"*, Jordan Publishing Ltd

[117]   An alternative design may be more beneficial in the long term

[118]   Chapter 9

or a right of access is requested, in which case surveyor(s) are appointed to determine the dispute.

3.10 Summary

Section 1 only applies where there is intention to build a "new" wall *"on"* or across the line of junction or executing repairs to an existing wall. Raising or altering an existing wall does not require notice and no rights under the Act flow from such works. The Adjoining Owner(s) cannot dissent to the works and the surveyor(s) are not appointed unless a dispute arises, in which case the procedures under section 10 will apply. To obtain access rights the existing structure can be demolished and rebuilt as a new wall subject to a valid section 1(5) notice. A wall can only be built astride the line of junction by consent.

There is a right to place projecting (but not special) foundations on to the Adjoining Owner(s) land without consent. In the event that damage is caused, the Adjoining Owner(s) are protected under the Act. If a dispute arises over the line of junction, the appointed surveyor(s) have the right[119] to determine the position of the boundary for the purposes of bringing the dispute to its natural conclusion with the service of an award. It is then a matter for the aggrieved owner to challenge the determination by way of an appeal[120] projecting foundations onto an Adjoining Owner(s) land can create easements and other potential legal issues and obligations that could be avoided by designing the foundations so that the wall can be built on the line of junction without projecting onto the Adjoining Owner(s) land.

---

[119] Loost v Kremer [1997] West London County Court 12 May (Unreported)

[120] Chapter 12 *para* 12.19

Chapter 4   Section 2—Boundary Wall, Party Fence Wall or external wall of a building

4.1   Introduction

This section deals with the *"Party wall"* because a party wall has joint benefits, ownership, and or liabilities neither owner is entitled to do any works without first notifying the other owner(s) of their intentions. It is therefore important that the appropriate sub-sections of the Act are identified and incorporated within the originating notice if served by a professional, (the layman Building Owner(s) preparing their own notices may be given some latitude if a challenge on validity arises) to avoid confusion and for the Adjoining Owner(s) to make an informed decision about what response and or counter notice should be served.

4.2   Application

s.2(1)

2(1) This section applies where lands of different owners adjoin and at the line of junction the said lands are built on or a boundary wall, being a party fence wall or the external wall of a building, has been erected.

EXPLANATION

Helpfully, earlier legislation and legal precedents[121] recognised that two types of party wall referred to under the Act are either a type (a) or type (b) exist and free standing walls may cross the line of junction. The complexity of this section is further demonstrated by the 13 sub-sections which allow various activities and careful consideration must be given when preparing the notice.

4.3   Owners Rights

(2)   A building owner shall have the following rights—

(a)   to underpin, thicken or raise a party structure, a party fence wall, or an external wall which belongs to the building owner and is built against a party structure fence wall;

EXPLANATION

The distinction between the two types of party wall, or party fence wall is dependent on the walls position in relation to the line of junction (see figures 1-5) and the walls function. A type (a) party wall is built astride the line of junction and not necessarily enclosed on both sides (see figure 7) or is enclosed upon on both sides (see figures 8, 9, 10, and 11). A type (b) party wall is wholly within one owner(s) land but has been enclosed upon to some extent either by agreement or through covert activities (see figure 12, 13 and14). Only the area of a wall within the enclosing structure is a type (b) party wall. The Act does not apply or afford any other rights on the encroaching owner(s) to the parts of the

---

[121]   Drury v Army & Navy Auxiliary Cooperative Supply Ltd (1896) 2 QB 271

wall which are across the line of junction or are not within the enclosed structure other than any easements[122] and/or rights at common law. I do not believe that the enclosing[123] owner(s) have the right to raise a type (b) (see figure 13) party wall because this would be a further trespass onto the Building Owner(s) land unless there was an explicit agreement[124] for the air space above to be adopted by the encroaching owner.

Where there is a necessity to underpin either a type (a) or (b) party wall on account of a want of repair or defect such as subsidence section 6(1) will apply. If the underpinning scheme involves special foundations then written consent[125] is required, however the underpinning will also benefit the Adjoining Owner(s) so in reality they are unlikely to withhold consent. The liability for the cost of such works shall be determined[126] by the appointed surveyor(s). If the underpinning costs are increased because consent is withheld and a clear benefit is obtained by the Adjoining Owner(s) it would be appropriate (in my opinion) to award those additional costs against the Adjoining Owner(s).

Conversely, when the underpinning is ancillary to other works such as (i) raising a type (a) party wall, (ii) due to increased loads applied onto the party wall, (iii) construction of a basement, and for the sole benefit of the Building Owner(s) in my opinion the costs should be awarded against the Building Owner(s). If the works involve special foundations written consent[127] must be obtained, and the costs (if consent is given) of these works must fall upon the Building Owner(s), if consent is refused

---

[122] Chapter 11
[123] Subservient
[124] Chapter 1 *para* 1.3
[125] Chapter 9 *para* 9.5 and Chapter 22
[126] Chapter 13 *para* 13.2
[127] Chapter 22

the increased costs for producing an alternative scheme will remain with the Building Owner(s).

Where an owner intends to raise the party wall or party fence wall they are entitled if they so wish to raise it for any part of its width.[128] The Adjoining Owner(s) cannot limit the raised section of the wall to the line of junction, the owner(s) are tenants in common[129] and can use the wall as necessary to complete their building activities. However, some party wall surveyors believe that if the party wall is raised; it must be for its full width. I do not support that view. As long as the raised section of wall complies with the relevant statutory provisions[130] the wall can be any width. If the proposed wall has to be wider than the existing, the increase must project into the Building Owner(s) property unless the Adjoining Owner(s) consent to having the raised wall positioned equally between the two properties. The Act is silent on raising the party wall downwards for a basement which is unhelpful.[131]

4.3.1   Repairs to the Party wall

(b)   to make good, repair, or demolish and rebuild, a party structure or party fence wall in a case where such work is necessary on account of defect or want of repair of the structure or wall;

EXPLANATION

There can be no reasonable grounds for either of the owner(s) to dispute the need to make good, repair or demolish, and rebuild (if that is the only

---

[128]   Bennett v Harrod's Stores Ltd (1907) The Builder, Dec 7 P.624
[129]   Cubitt v Porter (1828) 8BC 256
[130]   Chapter 9 *para* 9.6
[131]   Chapter 22

economical means of repairing the wall) because it will be for the benefit of all the owners. However, there is some difficulty in identifying whether this section applies to a type (b) party wall. The subservient owner(s) that are encroaching onto the dominant owners land can only have rights to enforce repairs of the section of wall that is enclosed upon (see figure 14) or unless they can establish for example that a right of support[132] exists. In Sachs v Jones[133] one house suffered from subsidence and dragged the other over. The owner(s) claim for damages failed because there was no obligation on the defendant to keep his house in good repair and the defendant had done nothing to cause the damage. This seems rather perverse, given that a right of support existed although this obligation may now have been addressed since 1980 with introduction of a measured duty of care.

4.3.2   Partitions

(c)   to demolish a partition which separates buildings belonging to different owners but does not conform with statutory requirements and to build instead a party wall which does so conform;

EXPLANATION

The word "partition" in this respect is confusing if not contradictory[134] in my opinion a partition that separates buildings belonging to different owner(s) must by definition either be a type (a) or (b) party wall. The materials used to construct the partition will not influence the status of the wall and this sub-section must therefore be limited to new works which will materially affect the existing (partition) party wall. The building regulations cannot be applied retrospectively, so any works to

---

[132]   Selby v Whitbread & Co [1917] 1 KB 736 and Chapter 11
[133]   Sachs v Jones [1925] AER 514
[134]   Chapter 2 *para* 2.12

upgrade the existing (partition) party wall must be as a direct result of other works executed by the Building Owner(s) and therefore must be responsible for all of the costs associated with the works under the Act.

4.3.3   Connections

(d) in the case of buildings connected by arches or structures over public ways or over passages belonging to other persons, to demolish the whole or part of such buildings, arches or structures which do not conform with statutory requirements and to rebuild them so that they do so conform;

EXPLANATION

An owner may demolish a part of a structure (over public highways or passages under third party ownership) commonly known as a *"flying freehold"* situation but must rebuild[135] them unless there is an agreement between the owner(s) for the permanent removal.

4.3.4   Reconstruction

(e) to demolish a party structure which is of insufficient strength or height for the purposes of any intended building of the building owner and to rebuild it of sufficient strength or height for the said purposes (including rebuilding to a lesser height or thickness where the rebuilt structure is of sufficient strength and height for the purposes of any Adjoining Owner);

---

[135] Chapter 11 *para* 11.5

EXPLANATION

It will be a matter of fact whether the party structure is or is not of sufficient strength or height. The Building Owner(s) would have to produce either structural calculations or a dangerous structure notice to demonstrate that the party structure was inadequate for its purpose. In these situations, the Building Owner(s) will be obliged to comply with any request the Adjoining Owner(s)[136] make including a request for security of expenses[137] before the commencement of any works.

4.3.5　Penetrating the wall

(f)　to cut into a party structure for any purpose (which may be or include the purpose of inserting a damp proof course);

EXPLANATION

The right to cut into a party structure exists for activities such as inserting *"Helifix"* reinforcing bars to strengthen the wall, or beam(s) and pad stones which are subject to service of notice. The example given of *"inserting a damp proof course"* is for illustration purposes only however, executing these works has given rise to some debate. There are of course several ways a retrospective damp proof course can be formed within a wall. The most common is to inject a chemical into pre-drilled holes which is then absorbed into the brickwork. Some surveyors suggest that drilling into the wall is not covered within this sub-section of the Act because the Act only allows an owner to *"cut into the wall"*. I do not consider that cutting into the wall is restricted to the use of a hammer and chisel or perhaps a grinding disc. Drilling is also

---

[136]　Chapter 9 *para* 9.2, 3 & 4
[137]　Chapter 14 *para* 14.2

a form of cutting, because the drill cuts into the masonry and therefore the two methods are not mutually exclusive.

Furthermore, it is unlikely that the Adjoining Owner(s) would object to these works because they benefit both owners. Although some older buildings may not have a damp proof course and these works may be deemed an improvement, and the Act is unclear if the Adjoining Owner(s) have to contribute[138] towards the costs of improving the wall. If the Adjoining Owner(s) can demonstrate that their property is not suffering from dampness they could avoid any liability for these costs.

Given the Act's specific reference to "inserting a damp proof course" it would be unwise for the surveyor to ignore the Act[139] when undertaking the necessary investigations to determine whether or not a retrospective damp proof course is indeed the proper remedy of repair. An important tool within the surveyor(s) and indeed all property manager's tool kit is the protimeter *"damp meter"*. It is an extremely foolish surveyor who conducts a damp survey of a property without the use of a moisture meter, but using it incorrectly or relying on the protimeter as a definitive tool for determining whether their clients should spend many thousands of pounds is equally as foolish.

The standard moisture meter has two prongs (approximately 15mm in length) which are placed onto the wall surface and pressed into the plaster to obtain readings. Inevitably the moisture meter prongs will not actually penetrate into the brickwork and only record moisture present within the plaster, identifying whether this is condensation or rising dampness requires more accurate tests. The proper test to establish the moisture content within masonry is the carbide *"speedy"* meter test, which provides a higher degree of accuracy and is probably the most

---

[138] Chapter 13 *para* 13.4

[139] Often dismissed as minor works

reliable and practical means of establishing the true or actual moisture content of a wall.[140] However, this approach involves drilling[141] into the wall and therefore raises the question of whether notice[142] should be served before commencing these investigations.

There are some surveyors that consider the nature of the works will determine whether notice should be served, suggesting that minor works such as cutting chasings into the wall, and speedy moisture meter investigations are *"de minimus"* and therefore can avoid the Act. I do not agree, the Act is explicit and places no minimum depths or requirements to determine when the Act should be applied. Irrespective of the purpose for penetrating the party wall the owner(s) should be advised by their surveyor to serve notice, the provisions of the Act cannot be ignored because the works are minimal.

The issue of cutting away plaster is another contentious area, whilst not actually penetrating the party wall I believe that notice should be served because it is not until the plaster is exposed that the condition of the wall is known. Pieces of the wall may fall away with the plaster or an over enthusiastic labourer may well cut in to the wall which could be construed as cutting into the wall. It is unlikely that dissent will occur, for minor works such as removing plaster, but it does provide the Adjoining Owner(s) with the opportunity to remove *"Uncle Percy's"* ashes from the shelf or any other important memento. Notwithstanding, it is simply good neighbourly manners and the same principles in respect of the service of notice for excavations, flows from the principle of reasonably foreseeable damage.

[140]   Birkinshaw, R. & Parrett, M. (2003) *"Diagnosing Damp"* RICS Business Services Ltd, P.79
[141]   Chapter 2 *para* 2.12
[142]   Chapter 4 *para* 4.3.5

The importance of serving notice can never be underestimated. In one party wall matter that I was involved with and having been appointed by the Adjoining Owner(s) to deal with the proposed excavations I asked the Building Owner(s) surveyor if there were any works to the party wall. The response was a resounding no, my Appointing Owner(s) who operated an art gallery arrived one morning to find most of the pieces of Art having fallen off the party wall, inevitably the unlawful cutting into the 102.5mm thick party wall for electrical chasings caused damage which ran into many thousands of pounds, which the Building Owner(s) were held liable for.

4.3.6   Cutting away from the party wall

(g)   to cut away from a party wall, party fence wall, external wall or boundary wall any footing or any projecting chimney breast, jamb or flue, or other projection on or over the land of the building owner in order to erect, raise or underpin any such wall or for any other purpose;

EXPLANATION

Before exercising any rights under this section, careful consideration has to be given to section 9.[143] The purpose of a footing[144] is clearly to provide support to a structure, and its partial removal must by definition be an interference with the right of support and or any other easements attached thereto, alternative works may be required and costs will inevitably flow from these works.

---

[143]   Chapter 11
[144]   Chapter 2 *para* 2.12

4.3.7   Cutting away overhanging elements

(h)   to cut away or demolish parts of any wall or building of an Adjoining Owner over hanging the land of the building owner or overhanging a party wall, to the extent that it is necessary to cut away or demolish parts to enable a vertical wall to be erected or raised against the wall or building of the Adjoining Owner;

EXPLANATION

If the Building Owner(s) are prevented from undertaking their works because part of the Adjoining Owner(s) property is overhanging the Building Owner(s) land they are in my opinion entitled to remove the projecting structure as necessary subject to the rights and obligations afforded under the Act.[145] It is not uncommon to find a situation (see figure 15) where part of one owner(s) gutters and/or eaves overhangs the boundary. Unfortunately, this will prevent the Building Owner(s) from building on or near to the line of junction. If we apply the principal held in Selby v Whitbread[146] the Building Owner(s) may cut away the overhanging section of the building and thereby removing the benefit from the easement so long as they are able to replace it with a different detail (see figure 16). The Adjoining Owner(s) would not have any reasonable legal argument to prevent this interference and the costs of executing these works would fall upon the Building Owner(s).

---

[145]   Chapter 4 *para* 4.6 and chapter 11
[146]   Chapter 11 *para* 11.5

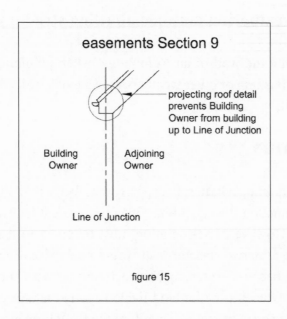

easements Section 9

projecting roof detail prevents Building Owner from building up to Line of Junction

Building Owner

Adjoining Owner

Line of Junction

figure 15

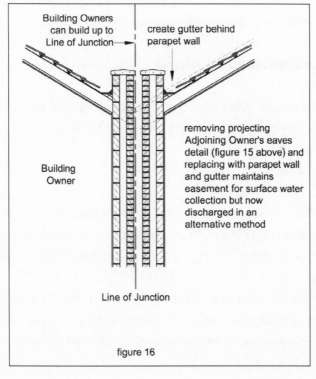

Building Owners can build up to Line of Junction

create gutter behind parapet wall

Building Owner

removing projecting Adjoining Owner's eaves detail (figure 15 above) and replacing with parapet wall and gutter maintains easement for surface water collection but now discharged in an alternative method

Line of Junction

figure 16

4.3.8   Weathering between abutting structures

(j)   to cut into the wall of an Adjoining Owner's building in order to insert a flashing or other weather-proofing of a wall erected against that wall;

EXPLANATION

When an Adjoining Owner(s) property has been built up to and on the line of junction, the Building Owner(s) are entitled to do exactly the same.[147] However, consideration must be given to the weathering detail between the two structures. It would be unwise to leave a gap of any distance because water could penetrate into both properties with the Building Owner(s) being held liable for any damage caused to the Adjoining Owner(s) property. Therefore the Building Owner(s) can cut into the existing wall and create a weatherproof detail.

4.3.9   Supplemental works

(k)   to execute any other necessary works incidental to the connection of a party structure with the premises adjoining it;

EXPLANATION

Including this sub-section within the originating notices provides the Building Owner(s) with a right to undertake unforeseen ancillary works without serving further notices and delaying the works. It is not always possible to identify the full extent of the works when the notices are initially prepared. However this sub-section invites wide interpretation and is often abused and used as a *"get out of jail"* card for additional works that should have been subject to the provisions of the Act.

---

[147]   Chapter 3 *para* 3.5

Accordingly, the ancillary works must be *"necessary works incidental to"* the originating notice. For example if notice has been given under section 2(2)(J) executing additional works under section 2(2)(g) are not *"incidental to"* these works and require a new notice is served.

4.3.10   Change of use

(l)   to raise a party fence wall, or to raise such a wall for use as a party wall, and to demolish a party fence wall and rebuild it as a party fence wall or as a party wall;

EXPLANATION

This sub-section is unfortunately not as clear as one would expect and is therefore open to abuse. The Adjoining Owner(s) do not always appreciate what they are consenting to and could having agreed to a party fence wall astride the line of junction entitle the Building Owner(s) to change the wall into a party wall at a later date. This may not have been anticipated and simply reinforces my opinion[148] that all agreements should be properly recorded. However, in the alternative, the Adjoining Owner(s) could if they wish also change the wall in to a party wall at a later date. It is important that the surveyor(s)[149] understand their duty to fully explain the consequences of any agreement that is made.

4.3.11   Demolition and reconstruction

(m)   subject to the provisions of section 11(7), to reduce, or to demolish and rebuild, a party wall or party fence wall to—

---

[148]   Chapter 1 *para* 1.3

[149]   Or legal advisors

(i) a height of not less than two metres where the wall is not used by an Adjoining Owner to any greater extent than a boundary wall; or

(ii) a height currently enclosed upon by the building of an Adjoining Owner;

EXPLANATION

I suspect that this section was introduced as a consequence of a decision reached in a landmark case under the earlier legislation where the surveyor(s) got just about everything wrong.[150] One of the surveyor(s) believed the courts decision was wrong and when participating in the drafting of the Act took the opportunity to clarify the position by introducing this explicit right for the owner(s) to alter the height of the wall. However, any alteration must not interfere with the Adjoining Owner(s) statutory rights and use of the wall.

4.3.12 Exposure

(n) to expose a party wall or party structure hitherto enclosed subject to providing adequate weathering.

EXPLANATION

Certain works will inevitably require exposure of the party wall and the Adjoining Owner(s) property. Furthermore, it is reasonably foreseeable that exposing the structure will increase the possibility of damage. The Building Owner(s) should not be deprived of exercising such rights, so long as the surveyors where appropriate include provisions to provide adequate weather proofing to protect the Adjoining Owner(s) from *inter*

---

[150] Gyle-Thompson v Wall Street (Properties) Ltd 1 WLR 123 [1974] 1 ALL ER 295

alia damage[151] and if the weathering subsequently fails the Adjoining Owner(s) are entitled to compensation.[152]

4.4   Chimneys and flues

s.2(3)

(3)   Where work mentioned in paragraph (a) of subsection (2) is not necessary on account of defect or want of repair of the structure or wall concerned, the right falling within that paragraph is exercisable.

   (a)   subject to making good all damage occasioned by the work to the adjoining premises or to their internal furnishings and decorations; and

   (b)   where the work is to a party structure or external wall, subject to carrying any relevant flues and chimney stacks up to such a height and in such materials as may be agreed between the building owner and the Adjoining Owner concerned, or in the event of a dispute, determined in accordance with section 10;

   and relevant flues and chimney stacks are those which belong to an Adjoining Owner and either form part of or rest on or against the party structure or external wall.

EXPLANATION

This section provides the Adjoining Owner(s) with peace of mind when the Building Owner(s) are undertaking works that create a material change to the chimney flues, chimneybreasts, and existing party

---

[151]   Chapter 14 *para* 14.2
[152]   Chapter 9

wall structure. The Building Owner(s) have an obligation to take all reasonable steps to ensure the works do not interfere[153] with or impede upon the Adjoining Owner(s) quiet enjoyment and use of their chimney flues, chimneybreasts, and existing party wall structure.

4.5   Liabilities and obligations under (2)(e)

s.2(4)

(4) The right falling within subsection (2)(e) is exercisable subject to—

(a)   making good all damage occasioned by the work to the adjoining premises or to their internal furnishings and decorations; and

(b)   carrying any relevant flues and chimney stacks up to such a height and in such materials as may be agreed between the building owner and the Adjoining Owner concerned or, in any event of dispute, determined in accordance with section 10;

and relevant flues and chimney stacks are those which belong to an Adjoining Owner and either form part of or rest on or against the party structure.

EXPLANATION

It is reasonably foreseeable that such works under section 2(2)(e) could cause damage and/or inconvenience to the Adjoining Owner(s) and whilst they are protected[154] this section simply reinforces their entitlement to compensation for any damage caused.

---

[153]   Chapter 11

[154]   Responsibility for damage is constantly referred to within various sections of the Act.

4.6   Damage under 2)(f) (g) or (h)

s.2(5)

(5)   Any right falling within subsection (2)(f), (g) or (h) is exercisable subject to making good all damage occasioned by the work to the Adjoining Owner(s) premises or to their internal furnishings and decorations.

EXPLANATION

This section simply reinforces the Building Owner(s) liability to compensate the Adjoining Owner(s) if damage occurs.

4.7   Damage under 2)(j)

s.2(6)

(6)   The right falling within subsection (2)(j) is exercisable subject to making good all damage occasioned by the work to the wall of the Adjoining Owner's building.

EXPLANATION

This section simply reinforces the Building Owner(s) liability to compensate the Adjoining Owner(s) if damage occurs.

4.8   Parapet walls

s.2(7)(a)&(b)

(7)   The right falling within subsection (2)(m) is exercisable subject to—

(a) reconstructing any parapet or replacing an existing parapet with another one; or

(b) constructing a parapet where one is needed but did not exist before.

EXPLANATION

The parapet wall provides two important functions (i) it establishes the location and existence of the party wall and (ii) forms a fire break between the properties. The location and position of the parapet wall is susceptible to greater deterioration and wear and tear than most parts of a building, especially on older buildings where porous bricks were used as a capping. The cost of reconstructing and indeed maintaining a wall above the roof line is obviously an expense that most property owner(s) would want to avoid. However this is an integral part of the party wall and therefore cannot (without agreement) be reduced[155] in height.[156]

4.9 Deemed statutory compliance

s.2(8)

(8) For the purposes of this section a building or structure which was erected before the day on which this Act was passed shall be deemed to conform with statutory requirements if it conforms with the statutes regulating buildings or structures on the date on which it was erected.

---

[155] Chapter 4 *para* 4.3.11
[156] Chapter 11

EXPLANATION

The building regulations cannot be applied retrospectively to any property, however if it can be demonstrated that the building did not comply with building regulations at the time of construction then any deemed compliance is removed and the Building Owner(s) could force certain works[157] because the structure will be deemed defective and obtain a financial contribution from the Adjoining Owner(s). Personally, establishing non-compliance in the first instance will be very difficult, but if the cost of the proposed works are substantial, the Building Owner(s) may invest time and money in investigating this option.

4.10 Summary

When preparing the notice, careful consideration must be given to the works and the relevant sub-sections of the Act that apply. Simply referring to section 2 is not sufficient for the professional because it would imply that the proposed works incorporate all of the sub-sections where in fact only a few may apply. However, if the layman Building Owner(s) prepare the notices absent of the sub-sections, so long as the intent is clear, they may successfully defend any challenges to the validity. Whilst I am mindful that this is an Act that enables owner(s) to interfere with the proprietary rights and legalise what are at common law unlawful activities, careful consideration must be given to the various sections before the surveyor(s) adopt them. They are not as straight forward as they first appear and any works executed under this section will undoubtedly have a significant impact on the Adjoining Owner(s) because of the direct link between the properties. Because there is a shared ownership, both owners have rights that cannot be superseded by the owner(s) works and in some instances these works will interfere

---

[157] Chapter 4 *para* 4.3

with easements which is contrary to section 9 but can be successfully achieved subject to applying the principles held in Selby v Whitbread.[158] Whether the Act imposes an obligation upon a property owner to have automatically transferred any subsequent rights to the area above the type (b) party wall) or a projecting part of the Adjoining Owner(s) building has not as far as I can establish been tested in law. For the avoidance of doubt I do not believe the subservient/encroaching owner can raise a type (b) party wall.

---

[158] Chapter 11 *para* 11.5

Chapter 5   Section 3—Party Structure Notices

5.1   Introduction

Quite why these sections are not incorporated at the beginning of section 2 will I believe remain a mystery, but we are where we are, and in moving forward, this relatively short chapter deals with the requirement to serve notice if it is intended to adopt any of the sub-sections of section 2.

5.2   Building Owners details and proposed works

s.3(1)(a)(b)&(c)

3(1) Before exercising any right conferred on him by section 2 a building owner shall serve on any Adjoining Owner a notice (in this Act referred to as a "party structure notice") stating—

(a)   the name and address of the building owner;

(b)   the nature and particulars of the proposed work including, in cases where the building owner proposed to construct special foundations, plans, sections and details of construction of the special foundations together with reasonable particulars of the loads to be carried thereby; and

(c)   the date on which the proposed work will begin.

EXPLANATION

It is important that the notice(s) for works[159] include the appropriate information, the absence of any of these elements will invalidate the notice.[160] *"The notice should be sufficiently clear and intelligible to enable the Adjoining Owner to decide what action to take"*.[161] The Adjoining owner(s) should be able to understand what the proposed works are and what (if any) counter-notice they should serve on the Building Owner(s). The notice should include such particulars of the proposed works as are reasonable and necessary at the time of preparing the notice. Interestingly, the Act requires the Building Owner(s) name, address and a description of the works, whilst remaining silent on the Adjoining Owner(s) details who can simply be referred to as the Owners[162].

5.3   Statutory notice and due diligence

s.3(2)(a)&(b)

(2)   A party structure notice shall—

   (a)   be served at least two months before the date on which the proposed work will begin;

   (b)   cease to have effect if the work to which it relates—

---

[159]   Chapter 4

[160]   Lehmann v Herman [1993] 1 EGLR 172, Patsalidies v Foye (2002) [unreported] HHJ RICH QC 29th October 2002], Gyle-Thompson v Wall Street (Properties) Ltd 1 WLR 123 [1974] 1 ALL ER 295, Crosby v Alhambra Co Ltd [1907] 1 Ch 295, Frances Holland School v Wassef [2001] 2 EGLR 88 et al

[161]   Hobbs, Hart & Co v Grover [1899] No. 1 Ch 11

[162]   Chapter 2 *para* 2.4

    (i)   has not begun within the period of twelve months beginning with the day on which the notice is served; and

   (ii)   is not prosecuted with due diligence.

EXPLANATION

Whilst the Adjoining Owner(s) are entitled to sufficient notice before commencement of the works, they are also protected from unnecessary delays. There is a general misconception amongst many surveyor(s) that the 12 month period starts from the date of the Award. Whilst the Act is explicit with the time period running from the date of the notice, if consent is given the notices expire. If dissent occurs the notices life expectancy has no limits until the award is served and the works are concluded. Once started if the works are not prosecuted with due diligence, the notice may expire and the whole process will start *de novo*.

Unfortunately, the difficulty arises with the interpretation of *"due diligence"* and in the absence of a statutory definition I have provided my own[163] in order to provide clarity and understanding. It must fall upon the surveyor(s) to consider the circumstances and reasonableness arising out of slow or non-progressive works. For example, if the Building Owner(s) after commencement the works, discovered unstable ground conditions, which delay the works because the foundations require redesigning or the increased costs requires further funding which takes time to arrange, would not be a failure to act with "due diligence". Unfortunately, the Adjoining Owner(s) may not be so sympathetic especially if their property has been laid open. The surveyor(s) would have to make a decision based on the degree of reasonableness and inconvenience when awarding any action and/or compensation arising from any delay.

---

[163]   Chapter 2 *para* 2.12

5.4 Lawful commencement without notice

s.3(3)(a)&(b)

(3) Nothing in this section shall—

(a) prevent a building owner from exercising with the consent in writing of the Adjoining Owners and of the adjoining occupiers any right conferred on him by section 2; or

(b) require a building owner to serve any party structure notice before complying with any notice served under statutory provisions relating to dangerous or neglected structures.

EXPLANATION

Para 5.3 *supra* ensures the Adjoining Owner(s) are not inconvenienced by the Building Owner(s) works whilst this sub-section provides the Building Owner(s) with the same protection and/or remedy once written consent has been given. The Adjoining Owner(s) are prevented from changing their mind at the last minute. In addition the Act is set aside if a dangerous structures notice is issued by the local authority. However, the Building Owner(s) can only execute works to make the structure safe with temporary supports or partial demolition. The works necessary to reinstate or repair the dangerous structure would where applicable require notice. It is the responsibility of the local authority building control service to take the necessary and reasonable enforcement proceedings to ensure the safety of any occupants or passers by. Building control surveyors will inspect all reported cases and deal with each case on their merits and degree of danger.

▪ If the property is in a deteriorated condition, but is not considered to be an immediate danger of collapse, a formal Dangerous Structure Notice will have to be served, giving the Building Owner(s) reasonable time to respond and offer a point of contact for further guidance.

- Where minor defects are found in properties the council will, if possible, carry out an inspection and offer informal advice on the best way of rectifying the problem.

- If the council need to take such action, they will make every effort to contact the Building Owner(s) in the first instance. If this is not possible, a card will be left at the premises indicating what action has had to be taken and who should be contacted for further advice.

- Where necessary the danger will be removed immediately by the councils own specialist contractors under the close supervision of an experienced senior building control officer who will ensure that the work is carried out in the most suitable way.

A dangerous building or structure can be anything on or about a building or structure that may be a perceived as an actual or perceived danger to members of the public such as:

- Loose or falling roof tiles;

- Roofs, walls and/or fences that are in danger of collapse;
- Unstable chimneys.

5.5 Summary

The Adjoining Owner(s) are entitled to two months notice before commencement of the works which provides sufficient time for them to decide what action and/or counter notice to take. When an award has been served the Adjoining Owner(s) can insist on the notice period passing before the works start. The notice(s) will naturally expire after twelve months if the works have not (i) been started within 12 months of the notice date and/or (ii) if the works do not proceed with due diligence. Once given the Adjoining Owner(s) cannot withdraw consent to frustrate or prevent the works from proceeding. The local authority can issue a dangerous structure notice which eliminates the requirement to serve notice. The Building Owner(s) cannot unilaterally determine that the building is in a dangerous condition to avoid the service of notice and/ or in any event where a dangerous notice has been served, the Building Owner(s) can only do what is reasonable to make the building safe, they cannot commence works that remain subject to the provisions of the Act.

Chapter 6   Section 4—Counter Notices

6.1 Introduction

The Act continues to recognise the Adjoining Owner(s) rights within this section by creating the opportunity to influence the design of certain works such as special foundations which the Building Owner(s) may not have anticipated when designing the project. The Act is silent on the liability for the costs incurred when undertaking these changes and is therefore a matter for the appointed surveyor(s) to determine. The principle of reasonableness will apply at all times.

6.2 Counter notice

s.4(1)(a)&(b)

4(1) An Adjoining Owner may, having been served with a party structure notice serve on the building owner a notice (in this Act referred to as a "counter notice") setting out—

(a) in respect of a party fence wall or party structure, a requirement that the building owner build in or on the wall or structure to which the notice relates such chimney copings, breasts, jambs or flues, or such piers or recesses or other like works, as may reasonably be required for the convenience of the Adjoining Owner.

    (b) in respect of special foundations to which the Adjoining Owner consents under section 7(4) below, a requirement that the special foundations—

        (i) be placed at a specified greater depth than that proposed by the building owner; or

        (ii) be constructed of sufficient strength to bear the load to be carried by columns of any intended building of the Adjoining Owner, or both.

EXPLANATION

The Adjoining Owner(s) counter notice may specify works that they consider are reasonably required to maintain the structure and integrity of the party structure[164] and/or party fence wall. Special foundations remain subject to the Adjoining Owner(s) written consent, and if given the Adjoining Owner(s) can influence their design and specification, e.g. in anticipation of any intended future works. Unfortunately, the Act is silent on who would be responsible for any additional costs incurred when accommodating changes to the notified works. In the absence of any specific obligation placed upon either of the owner(s) with regards to these costs, the surveyor(s) would have jurisdiction to determine liability for the reasonable costs.

6.3   Reasonable notice

s.4(2)(a)&(b)

(2) A counter notice shall—

---

[164]   Selby v Whitbread & Co [1917] 1 KB 736

(a) specify the works required by the notice to be executed and shall be accompanied by plans, sections and particulars of such works; and

(b) be served within the period of one month beginning with the day on which the party structure notice is served.

EXPLANATION

This reinforces the Adjoining Owner(s) duty to proceed efficiently and any counter notice[165] ought equally to be sufficiently clear and intelligible to allow the Building Owner(s) to make an informed decision on how to proceed. In some instances the Adjoining Owner(s) requests may be so outrageous that the Building Owner(s) may propose an alternative scheme to avoid special foundations. If there is any doubt about liability for the costs of the works the Adjoining Owner(s) could make it a condition upon consent[166] that the Building Owner(s) are liable for all of the costs on an indemnity basis.

6.4   Unreasonable requests

s.4(3)(a)(b)&(c)

(3) A building owner on whom a counter notice has been served shall comply with the requirements of the counter notice unless the execution of the works required by the counter notice would—

(a)   be injurious to him;

(b)   cause unnecessary inconvenience to him; or

(c)   cause unnecessary delay in the execution of the works pursuant to the party structure notice.

---

[165]   Should include drawings and specifications where appropriate

[166]   Chapter 1 *para* 1.3

EXPLANATION

This section prevents the Adjoining Owner(s) from requesting or demanding unreasonable and unnecessary works that force the Building Owner(s) to abandon their works. Deciding whether the counter notice is unreasonable will be a matter for the appointed surveyor(s) to determine.

6.5 Summary

This section provides the Adjoining Owner(s) with certain rights to reasonably influence the works within 1 month which avoids unnecessary delays for the Building Owner(s). If the counter notice is not served within time, the Adjoining Owner(s) are estopped from influencing the works. The Building Owner(s) are not obliged to execute the Adjoining Owner(s) works, and could proceed (excluding special foundations) if the surveyor(s) determine the reasonableness of the Building Owner(s) activities.

Chapter 7   Section 5—Response to a Notice

7.1   Introduction

This section continues to recognise the importance of time and of course anticipates situations where the Adjoining Owner(s) may not be receptive to the works and/or the possibility that the Adjoining Owner(s) simply cannot respond. The Act therefore provides a mechanism for moving forward.

7.2   Response to a notice

s.5

If an owner on whom a party structure notice or a counter notice has been served does not serve a notice indicating his consent to it within the period of fourteen days beginning with the day on which the party structure notice or counter notice was served, he shall be deemed to have dissented from the notice and a dispute shall be deemed to have arisen between the parties.

EXPLANATION

The Building Owner(s) cannot proceed until a response to the notice is received and it would be a ridiculous situation if the Building Owner(s) were left without any option but to wait for a response. In the absence of a response the Building Owner should add an additional 2 days onto the 14 days from the date the notices are consigned to the post[167] before the Building Owner(s) must deem dissent has occurred. The Building Owner(s) can only move forward if they serve a further notice.[168]

7.3 Summary

There is very little to add to the explanation *supra* when dissent or deemed dissent has arisen, the provisions under section 10 must be adopted. If the Building Owner(s) decide not to proceed with the works, the surveyor(s) are estopped from dealing with any matters other than the costs. There is nothing within the Act that says that the Adjoining Owner(s) cannot consent to the works after the 14 day period even when the surveyor(s) have been appointed. The statutory procedures of the Act simply cease, the only issues which the surveyor(s) can determine is the responsibility for any reasonable costs, which flow from the notice. An exchange of letters with fee accounts followed by payment brings all the matters to a conclusion. There is no reasonable or sensible justification for producing a formal award which only incurs further costs unless of course there is a dispute.

---

[167] CPR Part 6 Service of Documents r.6.26
[168] Chapter 12 *para* 12.6

Chapter 8   Section 6—Excavations

8.1   Introduction

Why should the Building Owner(s) have to inform the Adjoining Owner(s) that they want to excavate wholly within their own land? The justification flows from the principle of the natural right of support.[169] This section sets out the criteria that will determine if notice is required. The Building Owner(s) will obviously be concerned about costs and delays but the consequences of not serving notice far out way any perceived savings on costs and time.

8.2   Application of three meter notice

s.6(1)(a)&(b)

6(1) The section applies where—

   (a) a building owner proposes to excavate, or excavate for and erect a building or structure, within a distance of three metres measured horizontally from any part of a building or structure of an Adjoining Owner; and
   (b) any part of the proposed excavation, building or structure will within those three metres extend to a lower level than the level of the bottom of the foundations of the building or structure of the Adjoining Owner.

---

[169]   Chapter 11 *para* 11.5

EXPLANATION

Understanding where this section shall apply is best illustrated (see figure 17) however, whilst all other books on this subject illustrate this section with details of proposed foundations, the Act uses the word excavation and therefore applying the ordinary and natural meaning of *"excavation"*, I believe the statutory obligation to serve notice prior to excavating is not limited to foundations, excavations for drains, utility services, and/or reduction of the ground level[170] require notice, subject of course to the excavation extending to depth lower than the Adjoining Owner(s) foundations.

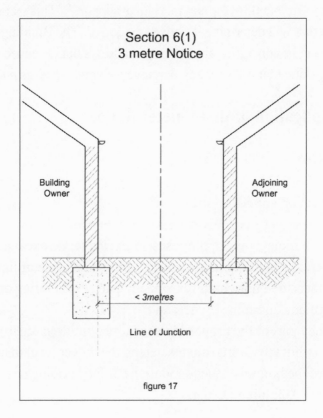

figure 17

---

[170]   Crowley v Rushmore Borough Council [2010] EWHC 2237

Where an owner intends to excavate wholly on his land and away from the Boundary, the structure placed upon it is not subject to notice. Once the foundations are completed the party wall surveyor(s) statutory appointment under section 6(1) or (2) below is concluded. It matters not, that the building owner(s) may be constructing a 25 storey building or a dwarf brick wall. The appointed surveyor(s) have no statutory duties in relation to the wall or structure. However, where there is an intention to build a wall *"on"* the line of junction the surveyor(s) jurisdiction remains until the completion of the wall.[171]

8.3   Application of six meter notice

s.6(2)(a)&(b)

(2) This section also applies where—

(a)   a building owner proposes to excavate, or excavate for and erect a building or structure, within a distance of six metres measured horizontally from any part of a building or structure of an Adjoining Owner; and

(b)   any part of the proposed excavation, building or structure will within those six metres meet a plane drawn downwards in the direction of the excavation, building or structure of the building owner at an angle of forty-five degrees to the horizontal from the line formed by the intersection of the plane of the level of the bottom of the foundations of the building or structure of the Adjoining Owner with the plane of the external face of the external wall of the building or structure of the Adjoining Owner.

---

[171]   Chapter 3 *para* 3.6

EXPLANATION

The same principles as explained in section 8.2 *supra* apply subject of course to satisfying the criteria illustrated (see figure 18). When considering whether notices should be served on blocks of apartments I believe the lease will dictate who should receive notice. If the lease places a liability upon all of the lessees to contribute towards the maintenance and repair of external fabric then they are in my opinion all Adjoining Owner(s) as defined under the Act and it matters not that their actual apartment may be outside the 3m or 6m distances set out in this section.

The foundation design will not dictate whether service of notice is required, for example piled foundations fall into two categories which are in laymen terms either (i) driven or (ii) replacement piles. The former drives the pile into the soil and the later removes the soil with the pile being inserted thereafter. Some surveyor(s) suggest that driven piles do not excavate the soil and therefore should not be subject to notice. Having debated this on several occasions I have not been persuaded to accept this argument. Logically and from a practical point of view I do not draw a distinction between the two definitions, a pile is by definition a foundation below ground level which must for the purposes of establishing if notice is required under the Act, involve a method of excavation in one form or another and is therefore subject to notice.

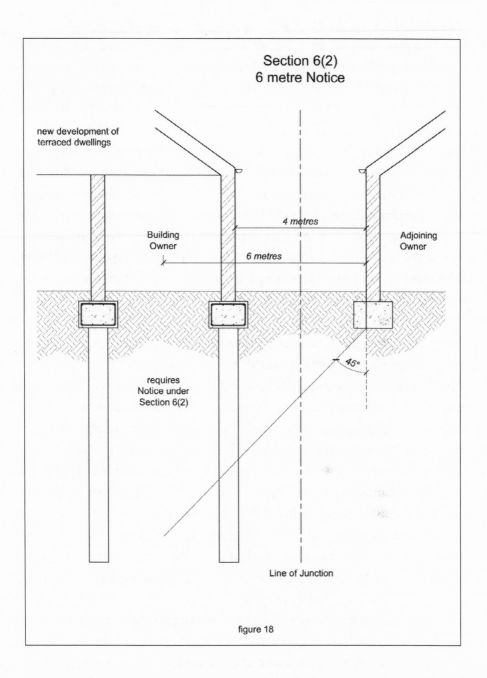

Section 6(2)
6 metre Notice

new development of
terraced dwellings

4 metres

Building
Owner

6 metres

Adjoining
Owner

45°

requires
Notice under
Section 6(2)

Line of Junction

figure 18

The distances as set out under section 6(1)&(2) are mandatory and not open to interpretation I have recently been involved with a very frustrating party wall project. Having been appointed by one of twenty six Adjoining Owner(s) I established after having carried out a site inspection that the proposed excavations were eleven meters away from the Adjoining Owner(s) property and therefore the Act did not apply, if we consider that the average cost of a party wall award for a large and complex central London development is £4000.00 for both the Building and Adjoining Owner(s) surveyor(s) professional fees, I had potentially saved the Building Owner(s) £112,000.00 by demonstrating that the Act was not applicable. When I brought this to the attention of the Building Owner(s) surveyor I was informed that many of the other Adjoining Owner(s) surveyor(s) had not raised an objection and that most of the awards had been completed and served.

Now this created an interesting situation because my measurements were either right or wrong and therefore simple enough to prove or disprove, if I was correct a large number of eminent surveyor(s) were going to be embarrassed, and indeed they were. They had no jurisdiction to produce any awards and had in my opinion been negligent when they failed to establish in the first instance whether the Act actually applied. However, the Building Owner(s) surveyor who is rightly or wrongly regarded as one of the country's leading authorities on the Act continued to demonstrate his failure to understand the jurisdiction of the Act when I submitted my nominal fees for the initial inspection and consideration of the notices. The Building Owner(s) surveyor rejected my fees and suggested I submit them to the Third Surveyor. I had to explain that because the notices were invalid the Third Surveyor did not have jurisdiction to determine the reasonableness or otherwise of my fees. Ultimately an account was sent to the Building Owner(s) with a full explanation of the situation and my fees paid in full. I believe the Building Owner(s) surveyor has been asked to refund all the costs they had incurred including the Adjoining Owner(s) costs.

8.4   Preventative Operations

s.6(3)

(3)   The building owner may, and if required by the Adjoining Owner shall, at his expense underpin or otherwise strengthen or safeguard the foundations of the building or structure of the Adjoining Owner so far as may be necessary.

EXPLANATION

It is a matter for the Owner(s) to determine (not the surveyors) whether it is reasonably foreseeable that damage may arise and request preventative works. The appointed surveyor(s) should give proper consideration to the proposed works and offer guidance. The appointed surveyor(s) cannot prevent the Adjoining Owner(s) from requesting these additional measures and the Building Owner(s) cannot avoid them if so requested. The cost of these works *"shall"* be borne by the Building Owner(s). However, the principle of reasonableness would apply and any dispute would then fall upon the appointed surveyor(s) to determine.

8.5   Definition

s.6(4)

(4) Where the buildings or structures of different owners are within the respective distances mentioned in subsections (1) and (2) the owners of those buildings or structures shall be deemed to be Adjoining Owners for the purposes of this section.

EXPLANATION

This helpfully establishes who is entitled to receive notice.

8.6 Reasonable Notice

s.6(5)

(5) In any case where this section applies the building owner shall, at least one month before beginning to excavate, or excavate for and erect a building or structure, serve on the Adjoining Owner a notice indicating his proposals and stating whether he proposes to underpin or otherwise strengthen or safeguard the foundations of the building or structure of the Adjoining Owner.

EXPLANATION

The Adjoining Owner(s) are entitled to reasonable notice before any works commence to allow them to consider what action and or advice is necessary. Any proposals the Building Owner(s) decides to implement to minimise the possibility of damage arising may have a significant impact on the Adjoining Owner(s) quiet enjoyment and may object. If the Adjoining Owner(s) object and/or prevent the Building Owner(s) from executing preventative measures to minimise or eliminate damage, the Adjoining Owner(s) will expose themselves to serious criticism not only from the surveyor(s) but also from the courts if damage does occur at a later date. The courts will always look at the parties' actions and apply the principle of reasonableness when deciding on the degree of liability and/or deciding on the appropriate compensation and make such reductions as they would deem necessary and reasonable. The appointed surveyor(s) can authorise by award reasonable works and if the Adjoining Owner(s) continue to obstruct the Building Owner(s) legal remedies can be initiated.[172]

---

[172] Chapter 18

8.7   Drawings, plans and sections

s.6(6)(a)&(b)

(6)   The notice referred to in subsection (5) shall be accompanied by plans and sections showing—

(a)   the site and depth of any excavation the building owner proposes to make;

(b)   if he proposes to erect a building or structure, its site.

EXPLANATION

This section is often to overlooked when preparing and serving notices, if drawings are not included, the notices will be deemed invalid because the Adjoining Owner(s) have not been provided with the appropriate information to allow an informed and intelligent decision about how the works will affect them, whether to consent, dissent and/or what if any counter-notices should be served. It would be extremely embarrassing for the party wall surveyor *"Professionals cannot afford to relax their standards"*[173] if they were to make such a fundamental error, but unfortunately it does happen. However, if the layman Building Owner(s) prepared the notices, they would be given some latitude providing the notice demonstrated the intent.

---

[173]   Manu v Euroview Investments Ltd [2008] 1 EGLR 165

8.8   Dissent

s.6(7)

(7)   If an owner on whom a notice referred to in subsection (5) has been served does not serve a notice indicating his consent to it within the period of fourteen days beginning with the day on which the notice referred to in subsection (5) was served, he shall be deemed to have dissented from the notice and a dispute shall be deemed to have arisen between the parties.

EXPLANATION

The Building Owner(s) are prevented from moving forward for fourteen days, until dissent or deemed dissent has occurred and serve a further notice[174] before the procedures under section 10 can be applied.[175]

8.9   Statutory notice and due diligence

s.6(8)(a)&(b)

(8)   The notice referred to in subsection (5) shall cease to have effect if the work to which the notice relates—

(a)   has not begun within the period of twelve months beginning with the day on which the notice was served; and

(b)   is not prosecuted with due diligence.

---

[174]   Chapter 12 *para* 12.6
[175]   Chapter 12 *para* 12.2

EXPLANATION

In 1905 the second[176] of two court cases arising out of party wall matters focussed on the question of the life expectancy of a party wall notice and established that a notice has life expectancy. Given the earlier litigation between the parties[177] the animosity between these parties was clearly evident. Marylebone served a further notice upon Leadbetter who refused to acknowledge and/or do anything with the notice until a further 10 day notice[178] was served under section 91(3) of the 1894 Act. The appointed surveyor(s) began to negotiate and discuss the issues, however for reasons which are not known these negotiations were protracted and after 6 months an award had not been agreed. Leadbetter immediately claimed that the time limit under section 90(4) of the 1894 Act[179] had passed and therefore the surveyor(s) were no longer appointed. Leadbetter's surveyor probably saw this as an ideal opportunity to step aside and walk away from what was clearly a very unpleasant situation.

Leadbetter was at first bite successful, however Marylebone appealed the decision and it was held that the time limit under section 90(4) applied where consent to the notices had been given by an Adjoining Owner. This would make perfect sense because it would be wholly unreasonable for the Adjoining Owner(s) to simply be left waiting for the works which they had consented to be undertaken. Where dissent has occurred and surveyor(s) appointed and moving forward with the issues which in this case were to regularise the matters which had been the basis of the first round of litigation it would be an absurdity if time constraints under the Act automatically determined the appointment of the surveyor(s).

---

[176] Leadbetter v Marylebone Corporation [No. 2] [1904] 2 KB 893
[177] Leadbetter v Marylebone Corporation [No. 1] [1904] 2 KB 893
[178] Chapter 12 *para* 12.6
[179] The London Building Act 1984

Helpfully, the current Act has addressed this issue by extending the notice period to 12 months, but even so this may not be sufficient to complete party wall matters on major projects and therefore time must reasonably be considered at large once dissent has occurred.

8.10 Amended drawings, plans and sections

s.6(9)

(9) On completion of any work executed in pursuance of this section the building owner shall if so requested by the Adjoining Owner supply him with particulars including plans and sections of the work.

EXPLANATION

This section is in reality seldom activated because the Adjoining Owner(s) would have had all of the drawings attached to the originating notice.[180] The only time where a requirement for further drawings arises is when the original works have changed substantially from the original works. However, there is no statutory obligation to provide these drawings unless requested to do so, and in any event, any request is limited to drawings relating to the works.[181]

8.11 Injury and loss

s.6(10)

(9) Nothing in this section shall relieve the building owner from any liability to which he would otherwise be subject for injury to any

---

[180] Chapter 8, *para* 8.7
[181] Chapter 3,4, and 8

Adjoining Owner or any adjoining occupier by reason of work executed by him.

EXPLANATION

There is very little to say on this section save for the obvious point that the Act continues to protect the Adjoining Owner(s) from any injury or loss caused by the Building Owner(s). However, the definition of *"injury"* has broad boundaries and the courts have recently included physical damage, economic loss, and psychological loss.[182]

8.12 Summary

Deciding whether notice is required will be determined by the information assumed or known about the depth of the Adjoining Owner(s) foundations. In many instances it is unlikely that there will be any documentary evidence, but in such circumstances a sensible and reasonable decision has to be made. The Building Owner(s) must serve notice on the Adjoining Owner(s) before commencing any excavations. The Adjoining Owner(s) are entitled to dissent[183] and protect themselves from any reasonably foreseeable damage. In my opinion excavations for any purpose that extend to a depth greater than that of the Adjoining Owner(s) building and/or structure within either 3m or 6m[184] require notice. I do not distinguish between an Adjoining Owner(s) drains, or pavement, a garage base or a block paved driveway when applying the Acts definition of *"artificially formed structure"*. Although a degree of reasonableness has to be applied and in most instances dissent from such works would not occur, but as can be seen from the Crowley case even shallow excavations can have a devastating effect on the Adjoining

---

[182] Jones & Lovegrove v Ruth & Ruth [2012] EWHC 1538.

[183] Remember dissent is not the same as dispute.

[184] See figures 17 & 18

Owner(s). The Building Owner(s) will have an on-going liability to the Adjoining Owner(s) for any loss arising out of the works which may extend beyond completion of the excavations. If consent is given the works must be commenced within 12 months, where dissent arises time is at large providing the surveyor(s) are diligently dealing with the matters.

Chapter 9   Section 7—Inconvenience and Compensation

9.1 Introduction

It is an unfortunate reality that building works of any type will be inconvenient and noisy however in certain circumstances it may be reasonable to award compensation. Deciding on what is a reasonable level of compensation has previously proved difficult to establish. Accordingly, the conduct of the parties will always play a significant part in the determination of compensation. Although, the surveyor(s) must remember that at all times their jurisdiction is limited to the works that are subject to the notice.[185] Any inconvenience from activities outside of the Act is not within their jurisdiction to determine.

9.2 Unnecessary inconvenience

s.7(1)

7(1) A building owner shall not exercise any right conferred on him by this Act in such a manner or at such time as to cause unnecessary inconvenience to any Adjoining Owner or to any adjoining occupier.

---

[185]   Section 1, 2 and 6 works

EXPLANATION

Establishing whether the activity being executed is unnecessary or inconvenient is difficult because of the circumstances surrounding each project will be unique and therefore becomes a matter of opinion. Whilst typing this section I can hear a cement mixer and pneumatic drills from a site three doors away from my office, I don't like it but I cannot actually say it is inconvenient and unnecessary or indeed unreasonable. These are normal building activities and in any event it is 10.30 am and the contractors are entitled to earn a living, so it all comes down to adopting a pragmatic and reasonable approach.[186] These activities and equipment creates noise but whether it constitutes noisy work and therefore a breach under the Act is very difficult to define given the nature of the construction industry.

In some instances it might be favourable to the Adjoining Owner(s) in commercial situations, that noisy works are carried out on a weekend when they are not necescarily open for business. Conversely, residential owner(s) may prefer noisy works are restricted to the week day when they are at work and not at home. However, noise is not the only activity that must be considered, increased vibration, traffic movement, parking and unloading, radios, shouting can all be inconvenient.[187] Therefore, each project must be determined on its own merits, and this requires a degree of common sense, reasonableness, and practicality between all parties including the surveyor(s). Unfortunately, section 7 is often overlooked when the surveyor(s) award rights of access.[188] which will by definition be more inconvenient to the Adjoining Owner(s) than perhaps noisy works.

---

[186] Emms v Polya [1973] 227 EG 1659

[187] Jones & Lovegrove v Ruth & Ruth [2012] EWHC 1538 and in the Court of Appeal [2011]

[188] Chapter 10 *para* 10.2 and 10.6

9.3   Loss and damage

s.7(2)

(2) The building owner shall compensate any adjoining owner and any adjoining occupier for any loss or damage which may result to any of them by reason of any work executed in pursuance of this Act.

EXPLANATION

This is a very powerful section of the Act because it entitles the Adjoining Owner(s) to receive compensation where loss or damage occurs from any work executed under the Act.[189] It was generally held that compensation should be limited to a quantified loss, for example, the physical cost of rebuilding a wall (if it was damaged). Further the surveyor(s) would apply the common law principal that damages will be assessed on the basis of making the innocent parties position (so far as they can do this) equivalent to what it would have been if the contract had been properly performed.[190]

In one party wall case I was involved in the Adjoining Owner(s) manufactured and serviced laser equipment. The Building Owner(s) demolished their existing building which was in any event outside of the Act but created inconvenience and a nuisance for the Adjoining Owner(s) resulting in a threatened legal action for interference to their business activities. To avoid litigation the Owner(s) sensibly agreed[191] that the appointed surveyor(s) would deal with this issue as soon as notices were served in respect of the piled foundations.

---

[189]   Adams v Marlebone Borough Council [1907] 2 KB 822

[190]   Murdoch, J. and Hughes, W. (1993) *"Construction contracts: law and Management"* E & FN Spon P.333

[191]   Chapter 1 *para* 1.4

There were two issues that had to be determined firstly (i) whether the vibration had and will interfere with the ordinary commercial activities of the Adjoining Owner(s) by applying the ordinary and natural meaning of the English language[192] and if the first was held to be a nuisance or inconvenience (ii) whether the forthcoming piling activities could be avoided and or minimised. In determining the first issue the surveyor(s) were mindful of the principals held[193] where *"an adjoining owner had no general right to compensation for loss of trade for work lawfully carried out"* and relied upon the decision reached in another judgement which turned on two very similar points. In relation to the first, it was agreed that the demolition were lawful works and although had caused an inconvenience, did not award damages.

With regard to the second issue it was agreed that the piling would create a nuisance or inconvenience that would materially affect the Adjoining Owner(s) business activities. It was agreed that if the Adjoining Owner(s) were prepared not to undertake any calibrating works on a Friday and Monday, the Building Owner(s) would bring their piling equipment onto the site and limit their work over several weekends. Fortunately the site was within an industrial area and therefore Saturday and Sunday working did not create any issues. A rate of compensation was agreed for the inconvenience and lost business caused by the proposed piled foundations which the appointed surveyor(s) based on an assessment of the Adjoining Owner(s) financial accounts calculated by a chartered accountant.

However, in a recent decision[194] the boundaries limiting compensation have been pushed further by the courts which now include compensation for damages, loss, and injury arising from the negligent or unreasonable execution of the building works. Furthermore, the claimant only has

---

[192]   Davies & Sleep v Wise [2006] Barnet County Court
[193]   Adams v Marlebone Borough Council [1907] 2 KB 822
[194]   Jones & Lovegrove v Ruth & Ruth [2012] EWHC 1538

to prove that the harassment was a foreseeable result of the intrusive activities. The Building Owner(s) were also the building contractor and having failed to serve notice, caused damage to the Adjoining Owner(s) property. They unnecessarily prolonged the works and played radios in the house and garden which created noise, failed to keep the Adjoining Owner(s) informed of their actions and trespassed by building an additional floor annexed onto the neighbouring property. The Adjoining Owner(s) suffered psychological injury and financial loss as they were unable to work, in addition to structural damage to their property. In the first hearing the Building Owner(s) successfully argued that they should not be liable for the injury or consequential loss of the Adjoining Owner(s) earnings because it was not reasonably foreseeable.

On appeal, the court clarified the test for damages, and held that the negligent conduct of building works did amount to harassment. This judgment sends a harrowing warning to all those Building Owner(s) that want to avoid serving a notice, and then consequently compounding the non-compliance by carrying out the works in such a way that amounts to harassment. *"It is a feature of this sad case that Mr Ruth throughout has failed to be open and transparent in relation to the time and scope of his building activities"*. The law is there to protect people and the courts will not sit idly by, when there is such a blatant disregard for the law. The law has sharp teeth and when it bites, it hurts, as can be seen in the value of damages circa £250,000 plus costs awarded the judgment.

9.4   Maintaining security

s.7(3)

(3)   Where a building owner in exercising any right conferred on him by this Act lays open any part of the adjoining land or building he shall at his own expense make and maintain so long as may be necessary a proper hoarding, shoring or fans or temporary construction for

the protection of the adjoining land or building and the security of any adjoining occupier.

EXPLANATION

The specific nature of the works will determine the reasonable degree of protection that must be provided particularly where laying open may include the removal of roof coverings, demolition of the party wall or part thereof, fence panels or other parts of the Adjoining Owner(s) property to achieve reasonable access. In such circumstances there can be no doubt the Building Owner(s) are responsible for maintaining and protecting the Adjoining Owner(s) property or land during the works. The surveyor(s) can award compensation[195] in respect of this disturbance and inconvenience.[196] The difficulty the surveyor(s) have is determining what is a *"fair allowance"*.

9.5　Special foundations

s.7(4)

(4)　Nothing in this Act shall authorise the building owner to place special foundations on land of an Adjoining Owner without his previous consent in writing.

EXPLANATION

Whilst the definition of special foundations[197] is universally accepted by all party wall surveyor(s) the Act does not specify how much reinforcement is required to make the transition from a foundation to

---

[195]　Chapter 13 *para* 13.5
[196]　Chapter 9 *para* 9.2
[197]　Chapter 2 *para* 2.6

a special foundation. It has been suggested that if a light weight mesh is introduced into the foundation but can be cut without affecting the integrity of the foundation it is not a special foundation. I take a different view, the introduction and purpose of any mesh must be to increase the structural integrity of the foundation, what other reason is there to include it. A builder will not insert a light weight mesh unless he is instructed and paid for doing so and the owner(s) will not instruct him unless advised by their structural engineer or perhaps by the local authority building control that it is necessary. Therefore assuming that someone has made a conscious decision that the mesh is (i) necessary and (ii) must be inserted into the concrete, it must in my opinion follow that its purpose, however minimal is to increase the foundations structural integrity and must by definition become a special foundation. When the Building Owner(s) intend to construct special foundations they must provide full details of the proposed works to the Adjoining Owner(s) who are not required to provide any reasons for withholding their consent and in such circumstances an alternative design must be adopted by the Building Owner(s).

9.6   Statutory approvals

s.7(5)

(5)   Any works executed in pursuance of this Act shall—

   (a)   comply with the provisions of statutory requirements; and
   (b)   be executed in accordance with such plans, sections and particulars as may be agreed between the owners or in the event of dispute determined in accordance with section 10;

and no deviation shall be made from those plans, sections and particulars except such as may be agreed between the owners (or surveyors acting on their behalf) or in the event of dispute determined in accordance with section 10.

EXPLANATION

Given that no deviation from the plans or sections can occur without agreement, it is not unreasonable for the surveyor(s) to undertake enquires with the local authority to establish if the proposed works have the appropriate statutory planning or building regulations approval. In my opinion, the surveyor(s) have both an implied and explicit duty of care to make the appropriate enquires with the local authorities to ensure that any works they authorise are lawful. The absence of any documentary evidence that confirms the statutory approvals have been obtained will entitle the surveyor(s) to refuse to sign the award without criticism or being exposed to an allegation that they have neglected or refused to act.[198] It is not a case of stepping into the local authority's shoes but ensuring that whatever interference with the proprietary rights the award may allow are lawful.

9.6.1   Permitted Development

This statutory right for certain works to be undertaken without planning permission has special interest in relation to both the Act and the Town & Country Planning (General Permitted Development Order) 1995. There have been conflicting interpretations on whether the GDPO would apply to section 2(2)(a) works. In a recent case,[199] the Adjoining Owner(s) objected to the raising of the party wall claiming that the GDPO only applied where the works were wholly within the curtillage of an owner(s) property. Accordingly, the Adjoining Owner(s) alleged

---

[198]   Chapter 12 *para* 12.8 &12.9
[199]   Planning Appeal Ref. APP/Q5300/X01/1062324

that without planning permission the proposed works were unlawful because half of the wall was on the Adjoining Owner(s) land.

Unfortunately, there is no statutory definition for the term 'curtillage' but it was held *"that for one piece of land or building to fall within the curtillage of another, the former must be so intimately associated with the latter as to lead to the conclusion that the former in truth forms part and parcel of the latter."*[200] It is hard to imagine that a structure which extends across the line of junction and clearly has an intimate association with two dwellings can be within the curtillage of a single property. However, the party wall must be considered an intrinsic element of both dwellings because an owner could not demolish the party wall without replacing it with an alternative structure because it could not function as such without it. *"Remove it and in all probability the remainder of the wall fails".*[201] Therefore, the party wall must by definition fall within the curtillage of both owner(s) property. It was therefore determined that where a wall extends across the boundary, it can for the purposes of the GPDO be considered to have satisfied the criteria of permitted development. Accordingly, if the proposed works do not require planning approval, the Building Owner(s) can proceed with the works even if the wall is in shared ownership.

9.7 Summary

The works must not create unnecessary inconvenience or nuisance. Unfortunately, building works are by their nature inconvenient and the degree of inconvenience will vary between projects and the parties affected by the works. Establishing what is or is not unnecessary inconvenience is a matter of reasonableness. The surveyor(s) have a

---

[200] Methuen-Campbell v Walters [1979] (1 QB 525 CA)
[201] *ibid,.* 192

"duty of care" to establish if compliance with statutory authorities has been obtained before signing an award and can in my opinion refuse to sign an award absent of such approvals without fear of criticism. There is nothing untoward or unprofessional in making these legitimate enquires.

In view of recent legal decisions, the sums that can be awarded for inconvenience, nuisance, damage, and the way in which the works are executed, are now open to wide interpretation. Building Owner(s) who press ahead with little regard to the consequences of "running over" the feelings of the local community are putting themselves in a precarious position. It is in the Building Owner(s) interest to ensure that they do everything possible to ensure that they and/or their agents conduct themselves in a manner that does not cause unreasonable or unnecessary inconvenience to the Adjoining Owner(s).

Chapter 10   Section 8—Access Rights

10.1 Introduction

This section will inevitably cause the greatest amount of concern, distress, and inconvenience to the Adjoining Owner(s).[202] The concept of section 8 is alien to the principle that an Englishman's home is his castle yet this section clearly provides the Building Owner(s) with the right to enter onto the Adjoining Owner(s) property, subject of course to demonstrating that the works must be *"in pursuance of this Act"*.

10.2 Achieving lawful access

s.8(1)

8(1) A building owner, his servants, agents and workmen may during usual working hours enter and remain on any land or premises for the purpose of executing any work in pursuance of this Act and may remove any furniture or fittings or take any other action necessary for that purpose.

EXPLANATION

It is reasonably foreseeable that access onto or through an Adjoining Owner(s) property will be disruptive and inconvenient. The surveyor(s)

---

[202]   Chapter 9 *para* 9.2

must remain open minded when assessing whether access is reasonable and justified, the following examples are illustrative of the issues that should be considered and unambiguously stated within the award.

The first, if not most obvious concern is that a right of access cannot be used to carry out ancillary works, so for example, whilst a new wall may be built on the line of junction[203] and require scaffolding to be positioned on the Adjoining Owner(s) land, the scaffolding cannot be used to facilitate the roof construction. As soon as the wall is completed, the scaffolding, and all other materials, plant etc must be removed unless a separate agreement has been reached between the owners[204]

The intention to project *"foundations"* onto an Adjoining Owner(s) property[205] will raise the question of reasonableness and necessity. In this context the activity being executed should be considered in careful detail, if an alternative foundation design avoids the need to project foundations and avoids access, the surveyor(s)[206] have a duty of care to award those alternative works. It is irrelevant that the alternative works may be more expensive or inconvenient to the Building Owner(s), the surveyor(s) primary duty is to minimise inconvenience and nuisance to the Adjoining Owner(s). If the Building Owner(s) require access for works of repair and maintenance they can serve notice[207] or initiate the procedures available within other statutory legislation[208]

---

203 Chapter 3 *para* 3.5
204 Chapter 1 *para* 1.3
205 Chapter 3 *para* 3.6
206 Chapter 9
207 Chapter 3
208 The Access to Neighbouring Land Act 1992

10.3 Forced access

s.8(2)

(2) If the premises are closed, the building owner, his agents and workmen may, if accompanied by a constable or other police officer, break open any fences or doors in order to enter the premises.

EXPLANATION

The only time that I have ever heard of this section being applied was in fact unlawful. An eminently qualified and well known party wall surveyor often recites (with pride) a situation, where with the attendance of a police officer he wanted access to the adjoining property. When the surveyor rang the doorbell, the door was answered and access was demanded and reinforced by the police officer. Unfortunately, the police officer had blindly accepted that what the surveyor had told him was lawful and in his most authorative *"hello, hello, hello"* tone advised the Adjoining Owner(s) to let the surveyor in. The police officer had not appreciated that section 8(2) only applies *"if the premises are closed"* the premises were obviously not closed and therefore the access was unlawful. This eminent surveyor accepts the point but still boasts to this day about his indiscretion without any shame or embarrassment.

The appointed surveyor(s) must be absolutely certain that they are acting lawfully if this section is adopted. In addition, where access is forced, it must naturally follow that the Building Owner(s) would be responsible for compensation[209] which may include *inter alia* (i) reinstating any damage caused, and (ii) maintaining the security of the Adjoining Owner(s) property until such time as the access is no longer

---

[209] Chapter 9

required. Furthermore, there is an implied obligation that the Building Owner(s) use reasonable force simply "battering" the door down when perhaps the use of a locksmith may afford a more reasonable means of access, must be applied at all times.

10.4 Access without notice

s.8(3)(a)&(b)

(3)   No land or premises may be entered by any person under subsection (1) unless the building owner serves on the owner and the occupier of the land or premises—

(a)   in case of emergency, such notice of the intention to enter as may be reasonably practicable;

(b)   in any other case, such notice of the intention to enter as complies with subsection (4).

EXPLANATION

In the case of an emergency, where notice is impractical forced access (similar to that afforded to the Fire Brigade) can be effected lawfully. The Building Owner(s) and/or their surveyor(s) should make absolutely sure that they can demonstrate the reasonableness of such actions otherwise the principles of common law loss, injury, and damages will apply[210] and or possibly expose them to criminal prosecution for unlawful entry.

---

[210]   Jones & Lovegrove v Ruth & Ruth [2012} EWHC 1538 and in the Court of Appeal [2011]

10.5 Reasonable notice

s.8(4)

(4) Notice complies with this subsection if it is served in a period of not less than fourteen days ending with the day of the proposed entry.

EXPLANATION

The purpose of serving a notice for non-urgent matters is to forewarn the Adjoining Owner(s) of the intention to enter onto their land. However, the notice does not grant an automatic right, if the Adjoining Owner(s) can demonstrate that the date of entry is inconvenient[211] they can[212] prevent access until a more convenient time. There are some that consider the 14 day period is unreasonable because it may unnecessarily delay the building works but I do not accept that position. All building projects require planning and the works requiring access should be scheduled into the programme. There should be no reason why the 14 day notice period is restrictive if the project managers have performed their duties correctly. It is not unreasonable to expect the Building Owner(s) and or his agents to actively communicate with the appointed surveyor(s).

10.6 Surveyors access

s.8(5)

(5) A surveyor appointed or selected under section 10 may during usual working hours enter and remain on any land or premises for

---

[211] Perhaps they are holding a family function on the day
[212] Chapter 9 *para 9.2*

the purpose of carrying out the object for which he is appointed or selected.

EXPLANATION

The difficulty with this section is defining the words *"usual working hours"* each project will be different and must be determined on their individual merits. What may or may not be usual working hours for some may not be for others.[213] It is also important to remember that this only applies to the works that are subject to the notice.

10.7 Emergency access

s.8(6)(a)&(b)

(6) No land or premises may be entered by a surveyor under subsection (5)]unless the building owner who is a party to the dispute concerned serves on the owner and the occupier of the land or premises—

(a) in case of emergency, such notice of the intention to enter as may be reasonably practicable;

(b) in any other case, such notice of the intention to enter as complies with subsection (4).

EXPLANATION

If the Building Owner(s) have not served notice of the intent to enter onto the Adjoining Owner(s) land, access can be refused.

---

[213] Shift workers may want minimum disruption in the morning

10.8 Schedule of Condition

This activity is not a mandatory requirement but given the broad remit[214] for the surveyor(s) to determine what is reasonable or not I believe it is sensible to produce a schedule. Those surveyors that engage in landlord and tenant matters will be familiar with the benefits that a schedule of condition provides. The schedule is also a double edged sword that protects both the Building Owner(s) from spurious claims of damage, and the Adjoining Owner(s) from allegations that certain damage pre-existed the commencement of the works. Given the importance and clear benefits to all of the owners and/or occupiers it seems bizarre that the Act did not incorporate this recognised and established activity within the Act. However, the schedule should include both a narrative and photographs of those arrears that may be reasonably affected by the works.

The Adjoining Owner(s) are not obliged to allow the production of a schedule and some surveyor(s) believe they do not have a right of access. I do not think that it is necessarily correct, the surveyor(s) have the jurisdiction under the Act to deal with *"any other matter arising out of or incidental to the dispute"*. Preparing a schedule of condition is a reasonable and necessary activity that is incidental to the dispute and could be an important document if damage is alleged and relevant to the surveyor(s) ability to determine the correct and reasonable level of loss or damage. Accordingly, it is my opinion that a surveyor could[215] obtain access by force (when closed) or where reasonable notice[216] is given.

---

[214]   Chapter 12 *para* 12, 14 & 15
[215]   Chapter 10 *para* 10.3
[216]   Chapter 10 *para* 10.5

The surveyor(s) owe a duty of care to all of the owner(s) and should implement the Act without discrimination to any owner, if the Adjoining Owner(s) refuses a lawful request for access, they could on conviction be guilty of offence.[217] Whilst this might appear extreme, I have been involved in party wall situations where Owner(s) have attempted to claim many thousands of pounds in damages with substantial costs incurred by both parties trying to resolve spurious claims. A schedule of condition would have prevented this claim from even getting off the ground. If the Adjoining Owner(s) refuse to co-operate the surveyor(s) should ensure that the Adjoining Owner(s) are fully informed that their refusal could prejudice or limit any potential valid claim for loss and damages. A full record of all requests for access should be retained.

10.9 Summary

A right of access only exists for *"works in pursuance of the act"* the paradox is that access will inevitably be inconvenient, given that the Building Owner(s) must not cause *"unnecessary inconvenience to the Adjoining Owner/Occupier"* how can the party wall surveyor(s) strike a happy medium. Access cannot be awarded for ancillary works unrelated to the Act but certain rights under *"the Access to Neighbouring land Act 1992"* may exist. If a property is closed, access can only be obtained with the attendance of a police officer. Where access is required reasonable notice must be served to minimise any inconvenience and can be prevented if inconvenient. If the Adjoining Owner(s) refuse access they could be guilty of an offence where reasonable notice is given. Access can be used for the preparation of a schedule of condition during normal working hours. In an emergency the Building Owner(s) can use reasonable force but remain liable for the security costs and compensation.

---

[217]   Chapter 18

Chapter 11 Section 9—Easements of Light and/or in relation to a party wall

11.1 Introduction

Invariably as with all legalisation, the boundaries are seldom cast in stone, and the Act is no exception. The inclusion of section 9 illustrates how the Act seeks to prevent conflict between its application and the expressed operation of the established law on easements. Unfortunately, in my experience this section is invariably overlooked by the party wall surveyor(s) simply because they do not fully understand or appreciate the importance of easements, what they are, and how the award may create an interference with the an easement. *"The relationship between existing easements and the operation of the statutes leading up to and including the 1996 Act has never been comprehensively analysed and understood and cannot operate without qualification"*.[218] Indeed, I had not fully appreciated how lacking my own understanding of this specialist area was until I had the pleasure of hearing Mr Christopher Cant present his paper on *"easements"* at a Party Wall Solutions Ltd[219] seminar that I was chairing. In just over one and a half hours I learnt more about easements than I had in four years at university and some 20

---

[218] Christopher Cant of 9 Stone Buildings is a barrister at law with nearly 40 years calling in general chancery and commercial practice.

[219] Chapter 1, *para* 1.7

years of professional practice and I have still only scrapped the surface of this interesting and complex area of law.

The party wall surveyor(s) should have an above average understanding of easements to be able to determine the issues under the Act. Having recognised my own limitations on the law of easements I am endeavouring to gather as much knowledge as possible about this fascinating area of law. It would be impossible to comprehensively address this topic within a single chapter suffice to say that those who wish to extend their understanding of this fascinating area of law are well advised to attend Christopher's seminar's and/or consider the recognised authority on easements.[220] The following is intended to illustrate the types of easements that the party wall surveyor(s) are likely to encounter, although it is not intended to be an exhaustive authority on the subject.

11.2 Interference of easements

s.9(a)&(b)

(9)   Nothing in this Act shall—

   (a)   authorise any interference with an easement of light or other easements in or relating to a party wall; or
   (b)   prejudicially affect any right of any person to preserve or restore any right of other thing in or connected with a party wall in case of the party wall being pulled down or rebuilt.

---

[220]   Gaunt, J.Q.C. and Morgan, P.C.C. (2002) *"Gale on Easements"* 7th Edition Sweet & Maxwell Ltd.

EXPLANATION

Section 9 limits the surveyor(s) jurisdiction to interfere with an easement, although that clearly cannot have been the Act's intention, because excavations[221] clearly interfere with the easement of support.[222] The surveyor(s) quasi-judicial position and statutory powers which allow an interference with an Adjoining Owner(s) property rights is further established under various sections of the Act. Easements come in all shapes and sizes, creating certain rights and restrictions *"easements as may be necessary to carry out what was the common intention of the parties with regard to the user of the wall".*[223] Understanding the complex intricacies of the law on easements must start with a definition, *"An easement is a right enjoyed by the owner of one piece of land over a piece of land owned by someone else".*[224] *There are two principle categories of easement; positive and negative. A positive easement entitles an owner to perform a "positive"* act on another owner(s) property, whilst a *"negative easement"* entitles an owner to prevent another owner performing an act on their land. It is an inevitable fact that issues with easements will arise whilst dealing with party wall matters and therefore certain rights and obligations will pre-exist for all owner(s).

There will be instances where easements may exist and apply where the Act does not apply. For example the construction of a 50 storey building more than 6m away from an Adjoining Owner(s) property does not invoke the procedures of the Act, but could still have a substantial effect on the Adjoining Owner(s) right of light. It is therefore important that

---

[221] Chapter 8 *para* 8.2 and 8.3
[222] Chapter 11. *para* 11.5
[223] Jones v Pritchard [1908] 1 Ch. 630
[224] Wood, D. Chynoweth, P. Adshead, A. and Mason, J. (2011) *'Law and the Built Environment'* Wiley-Blackwell P.196

the surveyor(s) recognise such issues and even if the Act does not apply they owe a duty of care to advise their owner(s) to take the appropriate specialist professional advice.

11.3 Right of Light

The nature of the right of light is in fact the same whether it is either claimed by prescription at common law, under statute, by implied and/ or lost grant.[225] Section 3 of The Prescription Act 1832 provides a mechanism which in practice is the most frequently used to establish a right of light, although seems to depend upon very different grounds, but can be distinguished between perpendicular and lateral light. The strict right of property entitles the owner(s) to so much light only as falls perpendicular on his land.[226] Although a land owner can acquire the right to lateral light without obstruction; such a right is an easement. In the absence of an easement an owner may build up to their land without fear of an action for interfering with the right of light.[227] However, if the owner(s) whose light is affected can demonstrate that they have enjoyed 20 years uninterrupted enjoyment of light[228] they will have adopted this right by prescription, but this approach does not apply to vacant and /or undeveloped land.[229] The importance of this provision is that the dominant owner is not required to demonstrate that his enjoyment of the light has been "as of right". Almost inevitably any works which involve raising a structure could potentially interfere with a right of light and it is incumbent upon the surveyor(s) to consider this particular aspect very carefully.

---

[225]   Chapter 1 *para* 1.3
[226]   Jones v Pritchard [1908] 1 Ch. 630
[227]   Chandler v Thompson (1811) 3 Camp. 80
[228]   The prescription Act 1832
[229]   Garritt v Sharp (1835) 3.A & E

There are surveyor(s) that specialise in rights of light, with an assessment process that involves a complicated series of measurements to assess the reduction in light. If a right of light is interfered with then the measure of damages will be dependent upon the loss suffered by the dominant owner. However, the principle when considering actionable interference does not automatically create a cause of action because there has been a reduction in the amount of light or an interference with the easement. The degree of interference will be relative to any actionable recovery for damages or loss arising from this interference. The decision in the House of Lords[230] and reinforced in a later case[231] established the basic principles that the measure of the light has to be seen and whether there is such a diminution as to cause a nuisance. If the amount of light remains is sufficient for the comfortable enjoyment of his property by the dominant owner(s) according to the ordinary notions of mankind there is no actionable interference.

11.4 Right of Way

Rights of way are one of the more familiar positive easements and are susceptible to an infinite variety that grants a neighbouring owner the right to move onto, over and/or across an Adjoining Owner(s) land. Whilst the easement may be created by agreement or by prescription[232] the surveyor(s) are entitled to determine a temporary right of way limited to "works in pursuance" under the Act and nothing else.[233] When awarding a right of access it is critical that the surveyor(s) determine and record the extent of the right which the dominant owner(s) will now temporarily enjoy over the Adjoining Owner(s) land.

---

230   Colls v Holmes and Colonial Stores (1894) 3 Ch. 659
231   Car-Saunder v Dick McNeil Associates Ltd) [1986] 1 WLR 922
232   The Prescription Act
233   Chapter 10, *para* 10.2

11.5 Right of Support

There are two types of right of support; the first is a natural right to lateral support of land which is clearly recognised with the inclusion of section 6 works. It is reasonably foreseeable that excavations to certain depths and within certain distances of an Adjoining Owner(s) structure could interfere with the natural right to support. If every owner of land were at liberty to excavate on their own land at pleasure and interfere with the lateral support without considering the neighbouring properties, it is inevitable that such action would eventually have dire consequences[234]. However, the natural right of support is only in relation to the land and not the building thereon.[235]

The second right of support is created either by grant or by prescription and can be provided by land or land and any building on it. Lord Selbourne held *"support to that which is artificially imposed upon land cannot exist 'ex jure natur' because the thing supported does not itself exist"*. However, if the land upon which it rests has been affected and damage is caused, and if it can be proven that the land has been deprived of its natural right of support damages may be recovered.

The Adjoining Owner(s) right of support was further illustrated[236] when it was held that the common law duty of a right of support can be replaced or discharged in a different manner by the statutory regime. One owner of a pair of adjoining properties decided to demolish their property and reconstruct it with the front elevation sitting approximately 13 feet[237] behind the front elevation of the Adjoining Owner(s) façade. This exposed the type (a) party wall to the elements requiring both

---

[234] Louis v Sadiq [1997] 1 EGLR 136; (1998) 59 Con LR 127

[235] Dalton v Argus (1881) 6 APP.CAS 740 at 792

[236] Selby v Whitbread & Co [1917] 1 KB 736

[237] 3.9m

temporary protection[238] during the works and a permanent protection after the replacement building was set back from the Adjoining Owner(s) front elevation.

The Adjoining Owner(s) claimed that they had enjoyed a right of support from the previous adjoining property and that the exposed section of wall was unsafe, due to the absence of the missing building. An award was made requiring the Building Owner(s) to construct a pillar or pier on the front corner of the building creating an alternative means of support. In effect the lawful interference with the right of support had not extinguished the original common law right of support but rather that the right was continued, but simply discharged it in a different manner.

There are numerous cases[239] that have considered the unlawful interference with the right of support and in one case the reduction of ground levels for paving works[240] which resulted in the collapse and/or partial collapse of the Adjoining Owner(s) property. In the latter case, it had not been anticipated that the reduction in ground level required notice under the Act. Whether this was through ignorance of the Act or because of a conscious decision based on an assumption of the depth of the Adjoining Owner(s) foundations that the reduction of the ground level did not require notice[241] is not clear from the judgment. However, the onus was on the Building Owner(s) to properly assess and if in doubt should have served notice.

---

[238] Chapter 9 *para* 9.4 and Chapter 11 *para* 11.8
[239] Louis v Sadiq [1997] 1 EGLR 136; (1998) 59 Con LR 127
[240] Crowley v Rushmore Borough Council [2010] EWHC 2237
[241] Chapter 8 *para* 8.2 & 8.3

11.6 Transferring an obligation to support

The right of support is two dimensional, existing both vertically or laterally[242] which is clearly recognised with the inclusion of excavation works and basements.[243] In the Rees case, cracking occurred but was not caused by the weight of the structure but by the effect of wind suction. It was held that it was not appropriate to distinguish between *"wind support"* and the more commonly accepted principle of *"weight support"*. Accordingly, an owner cannot transfer their obligations to provide or maintain a right of support without prior agreement and consent. I must confess it was not a situation that I had considered until the question was asked by Mr Edward Phillips[244] a surveyor who raised the following question: Can an owner of a mid-terraced house transfer their obligation to support adjoining properties onto other owner(s) without their consent?

The following example (figures 19, 20, and 21) demonstrates the situation clearly and without ambiguity. Property (a) shares a mutual right of support with property (b) and property (b) shares a mutual right of support with property (c). If property (b) suffers extensive damage and has to be demolished (figure 19) the surveyor(s) will have to recognise that property (a) and (c) has a right of support from property (b). There are two temporary methods of support (figures 20 and 21) deciding which method of support is acceptable must be determined by the principals held in case law. The surveyor(s) have to maintain the mutual support between (a) & (b), and (b) & (c).

If the scheme in figure 20 is adopted, property (b) obligation to support property (a) and (c) have been replaced by creating a mutual right

---

[242]   Rees v Skerrett [2001] 1 WLR 1541
[243]   Chapter 8 and Chapter 22
[244]   At a Party Wall Solutions Ltd CPD seminar.

of support between property (a) and (c). This interference with the easement of support is a clear breach of section 9 and therefore outside the appointed surveyor(s) jurisdiction unless the owner(s) of property (a) and (c) have consented. The surveyor(s) jurisdiction is therefore limited to the scheme in figure 21 which maintains the original obligations of support.

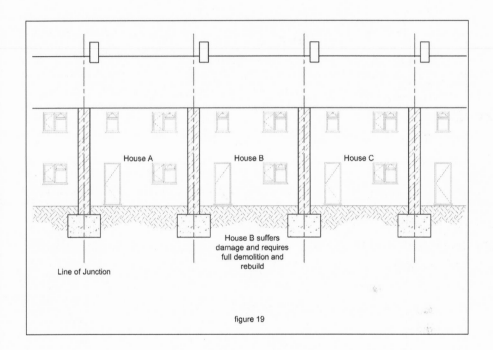

figure 19

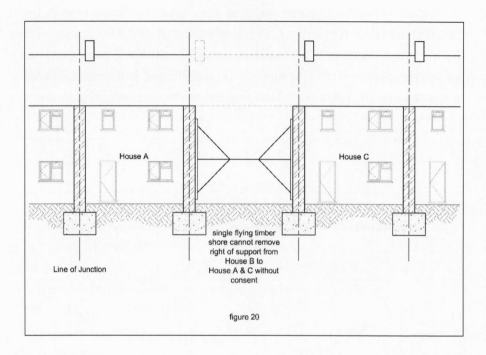

House A

House C

single flying timber
shore cannot remove
right of support from
House B to
House A & C without
consent

Line of Junction

figure 20

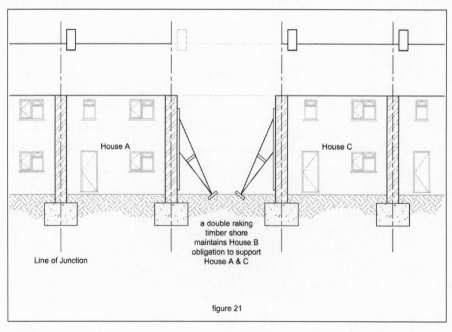

House A

House C

a double raking
timber shore
maintains House B
obligation to support
House A & C

Line of Junction

figure 21

11.7 Drainage Rights

This easement has a similar relationship with the rights to light and applies to both above and below ground drainage and arises independently from the wall but may have to be taken into account. For example where a gutter runs along the flank wall of a building currently overhanging the boundary line (see figure 15) an easement by prescription[245] may have been established. Whether or not the Building Owner(s) can remove the easement has been a matter of heated debate. In my view applying the principle held[246] the surveyor(s) are entitled to consider and award an alternative option that alters the existing construction detail so long as it is discharged in another manner.[247] As long as the alternative means of drainage is compliant with the appropriate statutory requirements (see figure 16) I see no reason why this alternative construction detail cannot be lawfully awarded under the Act. The Building Owner(s) will have maintained the easement and right to drain whilst removing the trespass across the boundary in a practical way that allows both owner(s) to enjoy their property rights.

11.8 Weather Protection

It was held that there was no easement to be protected from the weather.[248] However, there is an obligation under section 7(3) to provide adequate weathering when the Adjoining Owner(s) property is laid open[249] and is not distinguishable between either a temporary or permanent exposure. The principle of a measured duty of care reinforces this obligation. The decision in Selby v Whitbread further held that if an easement can be

---

[245] See figure 15

[246] Selby v Whitbread & Co [1917] 1 KB 736

[247] See figure 16

[248] Phipps v Pears [1964] 2 WLR 996

[249] Selby v Whitbread & Co [1917] 1 KB 736

altered but discharged in a different manner, the obligation to provide a permanent means of weathering must also follow.

11.9 Rights to Repair

As with other easements[250] the dominant owner is entitled to enter onto the servient owner(s) land to undertake works of repair and maintenance to drains,[251] water courses, and pipes[252]. The Adjoining Owner(s) cannot obstruct or physically prevent access or build over and/or cover the pipes either inadvertently or on purpose. If they do the courts will order the removal of the obstruction.[253] The access is of course always subject to the principles of reasonableness[254] and the primary legislation will ensure access is achieved. It is important to note that the dominant owner(s) are not under a duty to repair the pipe, but if he fails to do so, and the pipes contents leak on to the Adjoining Owner(s) land, the dominant owner(s) will be liable for the actionable tort of trespass and for any damage and/or loss caused.

11.10 Summary

This brief introduction to the law of easements demonstrates that it is a complicated and specialised area of law which clearly crosses boundaries with the Act. Therefore, before authorising any works under the Act, the surveyor(s) should undertake a careful assessment and identify whether any easements exist in relation to the proposed works. An easement will not necessarily prevent the works from being carried out if the

---

[250]   Chapter 10 *para* 10.2

[251]   Duke of Westminster v Guild [1985] 1 Q.B. 688 at 700E

[252]   Thurrock Grays & Tilbury Joint Sewage Board v E.J. & W. Goldsmith (1914) 79 J.P.17

[253]   Goodhart v Hyett (1884) 25 Ch.D. 182

[254]   Time of the day

surveyor(s) can determine a method that discharges it in a different manner. The interference will not necessarily create an actionable tort and in any event the loss must be measureable. Any interference with an easement or compensation determined by the surveyor(s) may be within their jurisdiction and subject to the right of appeal.[255] An award cannot transfer the obligation to provide a right of support to another owner without their consent and if in doubt the surveyor(s) are entitled to take appropriate legal advice on these legal issues and the costs can be awarded under the Act.

---

[255]   Chapter 12 *para* 12.9

Chapter 12   Section 10—Dispute Resolution Procedures

12.1 Introduction

If the Adjoining Owner(s) dissent or fail to respond to the notices, the Building Owner(s) must adopt the procedures within this section to be able to move matters forward. This section provides the statutory regime that establishes the appointed surveyor(s) jurisdiction to determine the dispute and will prevent matters from stalling. The procedures must be strictly followed to ensure valid determinations are made. The surveyor(s) that moves away from the explicit wording of the Act do so at their peril.

12.2 Appointment of the surveyor(s)

s.10(1)(a)&(b)

10(1) Where a dispute arises or is deemed to have arisen between a building owner and an Adjoining Owner in respect of any matter connected with any work to which this Act relates either—

(a)   both parties shall concur in the appointment of one surveyor (in this section referred to as an "agreed surveyor");or

(b)   each party shall appoint a surveyor and the two surveyors so appointed shall forthwith select a third surveyor (all of whom are in this section referred to as "the three surveyors").

EXPLANATION

Upon receipt of a notice the Adjoining Owner(s) have one decision to make which is either (i) consent or (ii) dissent. If they dissent they should either agree to the appointment of one surveyor who will act as the *"Agreed Surveyor"* or appoint their own surveyor.[256] The appointment of an Agreed Surveyor will seem an alien concept to the Adjoining Owner(s) because of the perceived conflict of interest. Members of the public really do not understand how this is possible, and they view the situation with suspicion, wrongly believing that the Agreed Surveyor will not protect their interest and rights under the Act. However, this statutory legislation not only allows one person to be appointed by agreement[257] it clearly encourages it.

The surveyor(s) have a statutory appointment which is unique and different from the traditional client/surveyor or agency relationship. The surveyor(s) will owe a *"duty of care"* to all owner(s) and occupier(s) irrespective of who appoints them and their role is to act impartially and assess the intended works to ensure compliance with the Act which allows those works to proceed without unreasonably interfering with the Adjoining Owner(s) proprietary rights.

If the Adjoining Owner(s) fail to appoint a surveyor the Building Owner(s) surveyor cannot appoint himself as the Agreed Surveyor. HHJ Pearl[258] clearly emphasised the importance of applying the ordinary and natural meaning of words. Accordingly, the natural meaning of "Agreed Surveyor" must reasonably flow from an agreement between the owner(s) and the absence of such an agreement in writing requires two surveyors to be appointed.

---

[256]   Chapter 2 *para* 2.10

[257]   Similar to a single joint expert

[258]   Davies & Sleep v Wise [2006] Barnet County Court

12.2.1 Selection of a Third surveyor

Following dissent to a notice, the surveyor(s) common law duties are replaced by the statutory regime and the two appointed surveyor(s) must forthwith select a Third Surveyor. The important word is *"forthwith"* which means immediately, the surveyors should not do anything until the tribunal has been completed. The word *" select"* is equally important because a Third Surveyor is not statutorily appointed and selecting the Third Surveyor requires a degree of flexibility by the surveyors. There is no prescribed format, but generally three surveyors are suggested by the Building Owner(s) Surveyor, the Adjoining Owner(s) Surveyor, can rejected all of the suggestions without any explanation and suggest alternatives which of course can also be rejected by the Building Owner(s) Surveyor without explanation.

Given that the definition of a surveyor[259] allows anyone to be appointed, it must follow that all three have a statutory and implied duty to apply the Act without favour to either owner(s) or surveyor(s) irrespective of their relationship with the Owner(s). The party wall surveying community is extremely small and it is inevitable that some relationships may have formed or exist not only through party wall matters, but perhaps from other general surveying and professional duties where paths have crossed. In my opinion these situations will not create a conflict of interest. [260] It is the surveyor(s) conduct that determines if a conflict exists based on their integrity and/or reasonableness of any decisions reached. In any event it is for the surveyor being selected to determine if a conflict of interest exists not the appointing surveyor(s).

---

[259]   Chapter 2 *para* 2.10
[260]   Chapter 12 *para* 12.2

Immediately after agreeing the selection of the Third Surveyor, the surveyor(s) should notify the Third Surveyor[261] of their selection before doing anything. The Third Surveyor may decline his selection and is not required to give an explanation. This advanced notice will prevent the Third Surveyor declining his selection, after a dispute has arisen. It is therefore good practice to ensure the tribunal has been properly selected. I have on two occasions been asked to agree the selection of a surveyor that had sadly passed away, when I pointed this out, the surveyor was rather embarrassed so make your nomination and selection carefully.

12.3 Once appointed always appointed

s.10(2)

(2) All appointments and selections made under this section shall be in writing and shall not be rescinded by either party.

EXPLANATION

The surveyor(s) appointment must be in writing[262] unfortunately there have been instances where surveyor(s) have proceeded without a valid letter of appointment, in such cases *"Everything is invalid and the whole process starts de novo".*[263] It is important that the surveyor(s) exchange their letters of appointment as soon as possible or provide them to the opposite Owner(s) although the Act is silent on this. *"The procedural requirements of the Act are important and the approach of surveyors to those requirements ought not to be casual. It would be a wise precaution for the surveyor of the Building Owner and the Surveyor of the Adjoining*

---

[261] Chapter 23 *para* 23.11

[262] Chapter 23 *para* 23.14

[263] Gyle-Thompson v Wall Street (Properties) Ltd 1 WLR 123 [1974] 1 ALL ER 295

Owner to inspect each other's written appointment before they perform their statutory functions"[264]

I have experienced situations where after 14 days have passed and deemed dissent has occurred, having adopted section 10(4) and following a further 10 days passing, appointed a surveyor on behalf of the Adjoining Owner(s), only to receive a telephone call from a surveyor claiming that he was appointed before the expiry of the section 10(4) notice. When asked why they had not notified myself of their appointment, they refer to the Act which only requires the Adjoining Owner(s) to appoint someone in writing and does not state that the appointed surveyor must notify the other surveyor of his appointment. If a surveyor withholds disclosure of their appointment they are not acting with transparency. The surveyor(s) duty is to resolve a dispute and to move matters forward, remaining silent on their appointment is (i) not in the spirit of the Act or (ii) a professional approach, and (iii) does not move the dispute forward. However, in reality the Building Owner(s) will have to decide whether to challenge this appointment or simply continue with him.

The letters of appointment must identify the surveyor because the appointment of a surveyor is personal. *"Under the Act it is quite clear that an individual has to be appointed. He has to be a person*[265] *(section 10(5)&(9)(c) reference to death) and under the Act there is the possibility catered for that he may die. It is absolutely clear that he must be an individual".*[266] Appointing ABZ Surveyors Ltd is not a valid appointment, as a matter of common sense and good practice letters of

---

[264] Gyle-Thompson v Wall Street (Properties) Ltd 1 WLR 123 [1974] 1 ALL ER 295

[265] Statutory appointment not agency

[266] Loost v Kremer [1997] West London County Court 12 May (Unreported)

appointment should be exchanged, as soon as possible how else would one establish the validity of the surveyors appointment.

The appointment cannot be rescinded which prevents the owner(s) from dismissing their surveyor(s) when they do not do as they command. It is inevitable that some neighbourly relationships will be less than friendly and in some circumstances outright hostilities may very well exist. The surveyor(s) are not social workers and should not allow themselves to be drawn into petty neighbourly disputes. Their statutory appointment requires them to resolve the dispute which flows from the notice and nothing else. Furthermore, the surveyor(s) must remember that they do not take instructions from the owner(s). Their duty is to remain impartial and apply the Act so that matters can progress to their natural conclusion.

I have experienced Adjoining Owner(s) telling me that they do not want the works to go ahead and that I must do everything to stop it at every opportunity. The only proper response for the Appointed Surveyor(s) is to tell the owner(s) that the Act will be applied without discrimination or favour to any party. The Adjoining Owner(s) cannot stop the Building Owner(s) from doing what they are lawfully entitled to do under the Act.

12.4 Conditional Appointments

Some surveyor(s) maintain that their appointment can only occur after service of a notice, I disagree, the acknowledgement notice will in any event state *"In the event of a dispute arising we/I will appoint Mr X as our surveyor"*.[267] This appointment is by definition a conditional appointment upon dissent which changes when dissent or deemed dissent occurs. Further *"an appointment under section 10(1)(b) can be made before the service of a party wall notice in respect of the*

---

[267]   Chapter 23 *para* 23.4 and 23.6

proposals to which it relates "[268] *and "the appointment . . . . Is put in that conditional way 'I would appoint' . . . ." The matter is quite sensibly put in terms of it being a conditional appointment".*[269] Accordingly, when the owner(s) are informed of the proposed works they can appoint a surveyor in anticipation of a notice. A conditional appointment will change in character when the mandatory provisions under the Act are invoked with the service of the notice(s) and followed by dissent.

12.5 Agreed surveyors failure to Act

s.10(3)(a)(b)(c)&(d)

(3) If an agreed surveyor—

(a) refuses to act;
(b) neglects to act for a period of ten days beginning with the day on which either party serves a request on him;
(c) dies before the dispute is settled; or
(d) becomes or deems himself incapable of acting,

the proceedings for settling such dispute shall begin *de novo*.

EXPLANATION

The Agreed Surveyor(s) appointment is extremely powerful, because he/she will have complete autonomy in dealing with the party wall matters. Unless the Building Owner(s) can demonstrate that the Agreed Surveyor has failed under sub-section (a), (b), or (d) above their only

---

[268] Manu v Euroview Investments Ltd [2008] 1 EGLR 165

[269] Loost v Kremer [1997] West London County Court 12 May (Unreported)

redress[270] is to appeal the award if they consider the award is wrong on any point. The Agreed Surveyor can at any time deem himself incapable of acting, however in my opinion they must have very solid reasons for doing so because the whole process begins de novo and this can have substantial implications on costs and delay the works from commencing because the whole process must start *de novo*.

12.6 Failure to appoint a surveyor

s10(4)(a)&(b)

(4)   If either party to the dispute—

(a)   refuses to appoint a surveyor under subsection (1)(b), or
(b)   neglects to appoint a surveyor under subsection (1)(b) for a period of ten days beginning with the day on which the other party serves a request on him,

the other party may make the appointment on his behalf.

EXPLANATION

I apologise for reiterating this point but it is important, the purpose of the Act is to ensure that works proceed without unnecessary delays or inconvenience and it is not unusual for owner(s) to ignore notices. The Building Owner(s) only option is to serve a further notice providing another 10 days for the Adjoining Owner(s) to appoint a surveyor. If they continue to remain silent, the Building Owner(s) can make an appointment on their behalf, but cannot appoint themselves as the Agreed Surveyor.

---

[270]   Chapter 12 *para* 12.19

12.7 Death or incapable

s.10(5)

(5) If, before the dispute is settled, a surveyor appointed under paragraph (b) of subsection (1) by a party to the dispute dies, or becomes or deems himself incapable of acting, the party who appointed him may appoint another surveyor in his place with the same power and authority.

EXPLANATION

If a surveyor dies, it is obviously necessary to appointment another surveyor, another surveyor from the same practice cannot automatically step in to the deceased's shoes. The same procedures for appointing the new surveyor apply[271] if the Adjoining Owner(s) have participated they are entitled to appoint a replacement surveyor. If section 10(4) was adopted, the Building Owner(s) Surveyor is entitled to make the new appointment. In my opinion the surveyor(s) should never deem themselves incapable of acting they should proceed and determine the issues with the service of an award and leave it for the aggrieved party to appeal the award if they so wish. Walking away from the situation is not helpful to any party and does not satisfy their professional and moral obligations to resolve the dispute.

The surveyor(s) owe a duty of care to all owner(s) and therefore I believe a surveyor must be able to demonstrate very good reasons for deeming himself incapable of acting. On a number of occasions I have experienced, the owner(s) being so hostile towards their surveyor that they have crumbled under the pressure and deemed themselves incapable

---

[271] Chapter 12, *para* 12.2

of acting. In these circumstances I would either proceed with the Third surveyor or act *ex parte*.

12.8 Refusal to Act

s.10(6)(a)&(b)

(6) If a surveyor—

(a) appointed under paragraph (b) of subsection (1) by a party to the dispute; or
(b) appointed under subsection (4) or (5),

refuses to act effectively, the surveyor of the other party may proceed to act *ex parte* and anything so done by him shall be as effectual as if he had been an agreed surveyor.

EXPLANATION

Acting *ex parte* is precarious to say the least, the pre-conditions that must exist to be able to exercise this power must be established. The surveyor has to be absolutely certain that they are entitled to proceed in this manner, and must be able to demonstrate that the other party has "refused" to act effectively. I would suggest that a fully recorded paper trail with all requests made in writing and proof of service etc to defend any challenge to the *"ex parte"* actions otherwise the award may be deemed a nullity.[272] A surveyor must also think very carefully before refusing to act because it gives the opposite surveyor the powers that would only exist as an Agreed surveyor[273] as demonstrated in Bansal v Myers.[274]

---

[272] Frances Holland School v Wassef [2001] 2 EGLR 88
[273] Chapter 12, *para* 12.2
[274] Bansal v Myers [2007] Romford County Court Unreported

In this case the Building Owner(s) Surveyor refused to deal with the Adjoining Owner(s) Surveyors fees, claiming that the Adjoining Owner(s) Surveyor should discuss them with the Building Owner(s). The Adjoining Owner(s) Surveyor proceeded *"ex parte"* awarding his fees in full. The Building Owner(s) appealed, HHJ Platt held that the Adjoining Owner(s) Surveyors *"ex parte"* award was valid because the Owner(s) play no part in determining the surveyor(s) fees.[275] It is important to note the surveyor(s) *"ex parte"* actions are limited to the request that has been refused and does not create an open license to deal with outstanding matters where no request has been made. The refusal to act can be applied to any activity within the Act. A letter wrongly asserting a noticed was invalid and demanding a new notice can (subject to earlier conduct) be interpreted as a refusal to Act[276] if the notice is subsequently held to be valid.

12.9 Neglect to Act

s.10(7)(a)&(b)

(7) If a surveyor—

    (a)   appointed under paragraph (b) of subsection (1) by a party to the dispute; or

    (b)   appointed under subsection (4) or (5),

    neglects to act effectively for a period of ten days beginning with the day on which either party or the surveyor of the other party serves a request on him, the surveyor of the other party may proceed to act *ex parte*, in respect of the subject matter of the request and anything so done by him shall be as effectual as if he had been an agreed surveyor.

---

[275]   Chapter 12, *para* 12.14

[276]   Manu v Euroview Investments Ltd [2008] 1 EGLR 165

EXPLANATION

There is one significant difference between section 10(6) & section 10(7), the latter requires ten days to pass before establishing a *"neglect"* to act which begins on the day[277] on which the surveyor has served the request. The request must be clear and free of ambiguity when served upon the other party to successfully defend a challenge to the right to proceed *"ex parte"*. The right to proceed *"ex parte"* is again limited to the request the surveyor has neglected to respond to. For example, if an Adjoining Owner(s) Surveyor has requested structural engineer's calculations to justify structural works on the party wall and the Building Owner(s) Surveyor has refused (for whatever reason), the Adjoining Owner(s) Surveyor has the authority to obtain structural engineers calculations. The surveyor cannot proceed with outstanding matters unless a further request followed by another 10 days and a further neglect to act occurs. The same stringent approach to recording the right to act *"ex parte"* must be adopted.

12.10 Failure to agree a Third Surveyor

s.10(8)(a)&(b)

(8) If either surveyor appointed under subsection (1)(b) by a party to the despite refuses to select a third surveyor under subsection (1) or (9), or neglects to do so for a period of ten days beginning with the day on which the other surveyor serves a request on him—

    (a)   the appointing officer; or

    (b)   in cases where the relevant appointing officer or his employer is a party to the dispute, the Secretary of State.

---

[277]   CPR Part 6 Service of Documents r.6.26

may on the application of either surveyor select a third surveyor who shall have the same power and authority as if he had been selected under subsection (1) or subsection (9).

EXPLANATION

Unfortunately, the reality is that the surveyor(s) may not be able to agree on the Third Surveyor.[278] This section ensures that the matters can proceed without any unnecessary delays occurring. The local authorities are now aware of their obligation to have an appointing officer and on the rare occasions that I have involved the local authority I have always written to the Head of Building Control. Where the local authority are the Adjoining Owner(s) the only option is to apply to the Secretary of State. Whilst I have never had to write to the Secretary of State I would anticipate that it would be a painfully slow process. When adopting section 10(8) I have always advised the appointing officer of the names of all the surveyor(s) previously considered and rejected by the surveyor(s) and asked for them to be excluded on the basis that this will only further increase concern and distrust however the appointing officer is at liberty to appoint anyone they so choose.

12.11 Third surveyors failure to act

s.10(9)(a)(b)&(c)

(9) If a third surveyor selected under subsection (1(b)—

(a) refuses to act;

---

[278] Chapter 12 *para* 12.2.1

(b) neglects to act for a period of ten days beginning with the day on which either party or the surveyor appointed by either party serves a request on him; or

(c) dies, or becomes or deems himself incapable of acting, before the dispute is settled,

the other two of the three surveyors shall forthwith select another surveyor in his place with the same power and authority.

EXPLANATION

The Third Surveyor is not immune from criticism and must act with impartiality and efficiency to prevent matters stalling. However, from my own personal experience I have found that some eminently respected Third Surveyors are extremely slow in dealing with referrals. To maintain momentum, when corresponding with the Third Surveyor I always serve a request under section 10(7) thus ensuring they deal with matters within ten days. However, they are likely to view such a request as a slight on their professionalism or efficiency, but I would not. The referring surveyor(s) are simply ensuring matters progress as quickly as possible.

Although, one has to be pragmatic, the Third Surveyor maybe waiting for submissions from one of the parties or for example an independent structural engineer to give assistance on a particular point. The principle here is that the Third Surveyor has a duty to proceed and must demonstrate this by informing the parties as quickly as possible of any issues which prevent them from bringing the referral to an early conclusion. When selected as the Third Surveyor, I will always include a section 10(7) request in any correspondence to the appointed surveyor(s) to prevent matters from stalling.

12.12 The Party Wall award

s.10(10)(a)&(b)

(10) The agreed surveyor or as the case may be the three surveyors or any two of them shall settle by award any matter—

(a) which is connected with any work to which this Act relates, and
(b) which is in dispute between the building owner and the Adjoining Owner.

EXPLANATION

The award may determine *"any matter"* connected to the work or in dispute[279] which gives the surveyor(s) very broad boundaries. The award can determine the manner in which the works are executed, responsibility of costs, rights of access, works to Adjoining Owner(s) property. The surveyor(s) must bring the dispute to a natural conclusion with the service of an award which is more in the nature of an expert determination than an arbitration award.[280] Any of the three surveyor(s) can produce an award for example an Adjoining Owner(s) Surveyor could bypass the Building Owner(s) surveyor and approach the Third Surveyor directly to settle by award any element in dispute. Once the award has been served, the surveyor(s) involvement is concluded save for anything which has been included within the award such as undertaking an interim or a final inspection and of course unless further issues arise after works have started such as damage is caused.

---

[279] The boundaries are therefore broad
[280] Chartered Society of Physiotherapy v Simmons Church Smiles [1995] 1 EGLR 155.

The surveyor(s) can if they consider it is reasonable issue several awards especially on large construction projects. For example, an award dealing with the excavations is not dependent on the flashing details having been agreed. Concluding the award on excavations allows the works to commence whilst outstanding points and details are discussed and agreed. This is acting with *"due diligence"* and efficiently if time is of the essence.

There is one rather bizarre practice that has been adopted by party wall surveyors for as long as I can remember but has never been addressed in any book on this subject and has always been a bone of contention between myself and other party wall surveyors. There is a generally held belief that once an award has been agreed the appointed surveyor(s) should retain unsigned copies of the award and only signed copies should be served on the appointing owner(s). An unsigned award has no value to anyone and it certainly could not be used in any enforcement proceedings.[281] Furthermore, given that the surveyor(s) have to sign at least two awards for each of the Appointing Owner(s) it matters not that they sign additional copies for their own files. If enforcement proceedings are required then the signed award must be used by their surveyor(s). The awards should then be served forthwith.[282]

12.12.1 Interim Inspections

It is quite common for the surveyor(s) to allow for interim inspections but they may not be reasonable or necessary. If the works are subject to the local authority approval inspecting the excavations prior to concreting will not require the appointed surveyor(s) involvement. If unforeseen problems arise, such as unstable ground conditions, which require the foundation depth to be increased, the Building Inspector will determine

---

[281] Chapter 17 *para* 1.2
[282] Chapter 12 *para* 12.17, Chapter 12 *para* 17.2

the appropriate depth and thus avoiding the cost(s) of a site inspection by the appointed surveyor(s). The party wall surveyor(s) cannot supersede any request that the local authority inspector makes because the works must[283] comply with any statutory requirements. However, I accept that there may be situations where interim inspections are reasonable and necessary, for example underpinning the party wall or exposing the party wall. In essence it is a matter for the surveyor(s) to adopt a pragmatic approach to a practical problem.

12.12.2 Retrospective Awards

There may be situations where for some reason the Building Owner(s) have commenced the works before having served a notice.[284] In such circumstances the works are outside of the statutory regime and are therefore unlawful. This point was held[285] in a case under the earlier[286] legislation involving building works to a basement (approximately 2.3m below ground level). The works had commenced on the basis that they were not subject to notice under the 1939 Act. Shortly thereafter Consolidated served a retrospective party structure notice and prior to the expiry of the 14-day notice period, the party wall collapsed. Surveyor(s) were appointed (after the event) and sought to determine the liability for the damage caused by the collapse but could not agree on liability. The Third Surveyor determined liability and awarded that Consolidated should pay damages to Woodhouse. Consolidated refused to pay the damages and the matter was appealed. It was held that the surveyor(s)[287] had no jurisdiction and therefore no statutory basis under

---

283 Chapter 9 *para* 9.6.1
284 Intentionally or through ignorance
285 Woodhouse v Consolidated Property Corp 1993, 1 EGLR 174
286 The London Building (Amendment) Act 1939
287 All three

section 55(k)[288] other than to determine the method, time, and execution of the works which followed the notices. The collapse of the party wall having preceded the crystallisation of the dispute[289] the appointment of the surveyor(s) was unlawful and therefore the Third Surveyor's Award was a nullity.

The consequence of undertaking works before an award is served, are subject to the common law regime and it must naturally follow that the surveyors do not have jurisdiction to make a retrospective award because the surveyor(s) statutory appointment does not establish jurisdiction to grant common law or equitable relief for the earlier trespass or nuisance.[290] However, if the owners jointly agree[291] the surveyor(s) can apply the Act retrospectively if so instructed.

12.12.3 Anticipated Awards

If the surveyor(s) have no legal jurisdiction to act retrospectively, it must follow that they do not have the jurisdiction to determine future works. The surveyor(s) jurisdiction only flows from a valid notice for the intended works or unless an agreement is made between the owner(s).[292] In Leadbetter v Marylebone[293] the surveyor(s) determined the right to carry out future works which were not subject to the notices. It was held that the appointed surveyor(s) have strict limited jurisdiction to decide on matters referred to in the notices and cannot have jurisdiction to adjudicate on future works. There are several reasons, but perhaps the most obvious is that anticipated works and awards may place a liability

---

[288] The London Building (Amendment) Act 1939

[289] Surveyors had not been appointed

[290] Reeves v Blake [2009] EWCA C iv 611

[291] Chapter 1 *para* 1.3

[292] Subject to notice under the act

[293] Leadbetter v Marylebone Corporation [No. 1] [1904] 2 KB 893

on a future owner, or interfere with their proprietary rights without their knowledge or participation. This point was further tested[294] when it was held that the surveyor(s) jurisdiction to award damages and/or compensation must flow from an actual loss and not a *"perceived"* or *"anticipated loss"* and are therefore not recoverable under the Act. In Midland Bank, it was anticipated that a wall might fail in 10-20 years and therefore sought to protect themselves from any future loss at the Building Owner(s) expense. The claim quite rightly failed.

12.12.4 Third Surveyor Award

The Third Surveyor should immediately upon receipt of a referral provide directions on how they intend to conduct the matter and also request certain information to establish the jurisdiction of all the surveyor(s). An experienced Third Surveyor should have a standard list of directions for the conduct and management of the dispute. Adopting the following[295] would be a sensible and pragmatic way to establish the ground rules and inform the owner(s) and surveyor(s) of their responsibilities and/or obligations.

The Third Surveyor should:

1) Request copies of all notices, letters of appointments, drawings and the agreement of the Third Surveyor to establish the validity of the Tribunal.

2) Request all documents, drawings, previous awards are disclosed.

3) Raise any initial questions regarding jurisdiction.

---

[294] Midland Bank plc v Bardgrove Property Services Ltd [1991] 2 EGLR 283

[295] Is not intended to be definitive.

4)   Ensure all submissions are simultaneously copied to the other party.

5)   The aggrieved party shall make full submissions to the Third Surveyor within 14 days of crystallisation[296] of the dispute.

6)   The responding party shall have 14 days to respond.

7)   If called upon the Third Surveyor will attend at the telephone and/or engage in conversations on the basis that they are open discussions, and the Third Surveyor will within 24 hours provide a full transcript of the discussion with the other side.

8)   On receipt of the parties submissions the Third Surveyor shall determine the dispute within 14 days or provide further directions where there is a need to seek clarification on any points, or where it may be necessary and appropriate to arrange a site inspection (case specific).

9)   The Third Surveyor reserves the right to seek the appropriate and necessary advice of third parties such as structural engineers, quantity surveyors, and/or legal advisers on certain points of law if appropriate.

10) The Third Surveyors award should simultaneously be served upon the owners and their surveyor(s) to ensure the fourteen day period of appeal commences simultaneously.

11) The parties may request the surveyor to vary the directions which will be considered on the merits of the request.

---

[296]   The date when the Third Surveyor accepts the dispute.

12.12.5 Addendum Awards

The appointed surveyor(s) can issue as many awards as they deem necessary to conclude matters if it allows the owner(s) to progress with certain aspect of the works. Delaying the process until all the decisions are reached is not necessarily reasonable or acting with due diligence. However this will increase costs so the owner(s) should be made aware of the consequences.

12.13 Third surveyor referrals

s.10(11)

(11) Either of the parties or either of the surveyors appointed by the parties may call upon the third surveyor selected in pursuant of this section to determine the disputed matters and he shall make the necessary award.

EXPLANATION

I am constantly amazed by the number of surveyor(s) who do not inform their Appointing Owner(s) of the identity and role of the Third Surveyor[297] or their rights to make a referral or other rights which exist within the Act.[298] Withholding this information prevents the owner(s) from exercising their lawful right to make a referral to the Third Surveyor. Disappointingly, in the majority of instances the first time the owners /occupiers are aware of the Third Surveyor's involvement is when they receive the award which is clearly unacceptable. The appointed surveyor(s) have a *"duty of care"* to advise the owner(s) of their rights and the procedures under the Act

---

[297] Chapter 12 *para* 12.13
[298] Chapter 14 *para* 14.2

The Third Surveyor is a quasi-arbitrator who receives submissions from the surveyor(s) or owner(s) (where appropriate) carry out site inspections to reach his determination. All disputes and/or referrals will vary in complexity and therefore require varying degrees of time to resolve. It may in some instances be possible for the Third Surveyor to resolve some of the issues in dispute and serve an award so that the works can proceed, whilst resolving those outstanding points which make take considerably more time to resolve.

The Third Surveyor has the same broad powers as the appointed surveyor(s) and can determine any matter and also apportion liability for the costs. It is reasonable to assume that the unsuccessful party may look for legal technicalities to invalidate the award accordingly the Third Surveyor should have this at the forefront of their mind and ensure they conduct matters with transparency, impartiality, and include within the award a detailed explanation of how they reached their determination[299] to avoid criticism. Unfortunately, for the Building Owner(s)[300] the court were left wanting for evidence that supported the Third Surveyor(s) determination and accordingly found in favour of the appellants.

12.14 Determination

s.10(12)(a)(b)&(c)

(12) An award may determine—

   (a)   the right to execute any work;
   (b)   the time and manner of executing any work; and
   (c)   any other matter arising out of or incidental to the dispute including the costs of making the award;

---

[299]   Bansal v Myers [2007] Romford County Court Unreported
[300]   Davies & Sleep v Wise [2006] Barnet County Court

but any period appointed by the award for executing any work shall not unless otherwise agreed between the building owner and the Adjoining Owner begin to run until after the expiration of the period prescribed by this Act for serve of the notice in respect of which the dispute raises or is deemed to have arisen.

EXPLANATION

This section illustrates the wide and broad powers that the appointed surveyor(s) have in determining "any other matters" arising out of the works, including their own fees. This is an alien concept to any commercial arrangement where there does not have to be a previously agreed fee or negotiation between the surveyor(s) and the owner(s). It simply falls upon the surveyor(s) to determine what they believe in their opinion is reasonable. There is no legal definition of *"reasonable"* and accordingly under the Act would turn on the merits of the case and the parties conduct.

The decision in Bansal v Myers helpfully reinforces the surveyor(s) jurisdiction to determine the reasonableness of their own fees.[301] The surveyor(s) should be proactive in all matters at all times. To simply say *"discuss it with the Building Owner"* was held unreasonable and either a refusal[302] or a neglect to act.[303] The Adjoining Owner(s) surveyor submitted fees to the Building Owner(s) Surveyor for his consideration. The Building Owner(s) surveyor claimed they were unreasonable and determined that it was a matter for the Building Owner(s) to agree the fees with the Adjoining Owner(s) Surveyor. Having been served with a notice under section 10(7) requesting a response, the Building Owner(s)

---

[301] Bickford-Smith, S. and Sydenham, C. 3rd ed, (2009) *"Party Walls Law and Practice"*, Jordan Publishing Ltd
[302] Chapter 12 *para* 12.8
[303] Chapter 12 *para* 12.9

Surveyor unfortunately did not provide a counter offer or suggest what he considered was reasonable. The Adjoining Owner(s) Surveyor acted "*ex parte*" and served an award. The award was appealed, but the court held that the costs were a matter for the surveyor(s) to determine and not the owner(s). The Building Owner(s) surveyor having neglected to provide reasoned objections on the submitted schedule of fees, accordingly the Adjoining Owner(s) surveyor was entitled to proceed "*ex parte*".

12.15 Reasonable costs

s.10(13)(a)(b)&(c)

(13) The reasonable costs incurred in—

    (a)   making or obtaining an award under this section;
    (b)   reasonable inspections of work to which the award relates; and
    (c)   any other matter arising out of the dispute,

shall be paid by such of the parties as the surveyor or surveyors making the award determine.

EXPLANATION

This section certainly reinforces the principle that the surveyor(s) can determine their own fees.[304] The surveyor(s) are under a statutory duty to deal with the matters as they consider reasonable and leave the aggrieved party to decide whether they wish to appeal the award. The Act generally places a responsibility on the Building Owner(s) to pay the reasonable costs and this is often seen as a way for the Adjoining Owner(s) to exploit the situation especially where the relationship is hostile. The

---

[304]   Chapter 12 *para* 12.14

appointed surveyor(s) must explain that this is not an opportunity for the Adjoining Owner(s) to create or impose unreasonable costs upon the Building Owner(s). However because money is such an emotive subject, especially where unforeseen costs have not been budgeted for, the Building Owner(s) initial response will be *"why do I have to pay for the Adjoining Owner(s) surveyors costs"*. The answer is relatively straightforward, because the Act legalises the Building Owner(s) right to interfere with the proprietary rights of the Adjoining Owner(s) who should not be exposed to costs because of the Building Owner(s) desire to do certain works.[305] It must reasonably and naturally follow that the Building Owner(s) should be responsible for the reasonable costs incurred by the parties.

This power to award costs extends to engineers fees, building costs for repairing damage, and other reasonable and proportionate disbursements incurred during the exercise of the surveyor(s) statutory duty. It has been held[306] that there may be circumstances in which the appointed surveyor(s) have the power to award payment of non-contentious legal costs.[307] The jurisdiction to award legal costs does have some limitations having been decided on the basis of contentious and non-contentious costs in a recent case where it was held *"there can be no doubt that there may be circumstances in which appointed surveyors have the power under section 10 to order payment by one adjoining owner of legal costs reasonably and properly incurred by another"*. [308]

---

[305] Chapter 3, 4 and 8

[306] Chapter 12 *para* 12.15

[307] Onigbanjo, A. v Mr & Mrs Pearson [2008] The Mayors and City of London Court

[308] Reeves v Blake [2009] EWCA C iv 611 P.14

In Reeves v Blake a second award authorised and directed the content, manner, and timing of work to be carried out by the respondent. In a letter sent to the respondent with the second award The surveyor said:

"It is regrettable that the works progressed without settlement of an award thus giving the Adjoining Owner little option other than to take legal advice and with the work continuing. To instigate proceedings to stop the work until such time as an award had been settled and delivered. Such a set of circumstances involve significant timing on the part of both surveyors and solicitors and per the terms of the award, are recoverable in accordance with section 10(13) of the Act. I enclose herewith the various fee accounts referred to in clause 9 of the award and would ask that these accounts be discharged directly. My own invoice will be rendered in due course".

The surveyor had awarded that the respondents forthwith pay the appellants solicitors legal fees of £7,651.49 + VAT. However, it was conceded on behalf of the appellant that all of those costs were in respect of *"contemplated proceedings"* for which draft particulars of claim and draft witness statements had been prepared, but which were never required.

Applying the principle that future or anticipated costs cannot be recovered[309] it seems bizarre that the legal advisors submitted a claim for these costs and that they were awarded. In simple terms the solicitors had "jumped the gun" in anticipation of litigation. It is explained[310] that surveyor(s) have the authority to deal with non-contentious legal costs. The surveyor(s) clearly got it wrong and authorised costs which they had no jurisdiction to do, which further demonstrates that surveyor(s)

---

[309]   Midland Bank plc v Bardgrove Property Services Ltd [1991] 2 EGLR 283
[310]   Chapter 13 *para* 13.3

should not operate outside their jurisdiction. The Act is a double edged sword and it is for the surveyor(s) to determine the reasonable fees and who will pay them. Ultimately someone could find themselves exposed to substantial costs.

12.16 Service of the award

s.10(14)

(14) Where the surveyors appointed by the parties make an award the surveyors shall serve it forthwith on the parties.

EXPLANATION

The surveyor(s) objective is to produce an award that allows works to proceed and once the surveyor(s) have agreed the award, they have to "forthwith" serve[311] it on the Appointing Owners which means immediately. The Award is an important legal document which authorises an interference with the proprietary rights of owner(s) and may place obligations in respect of costs and other matters on to a party. The Building Owner(s) surveyor will in normal and amicable circumstances prepare and send fair copies of the final award with any attachments which may include the agreed relevant drawings, a schedule of condition (if prepared) to the Adjoining Owner(s) surveyor for signature. However, this is where I believe the process of service becomes unnecessarily prolonged.

The Adjoining Owner(s) surveyor will normally sign and serve the award on his appointing owner(s) and return signed copies to the Building Owner(s) surveyor to serve the award upon the Building Owner(s). Given

---

[311]   Chapter 15, *para* 15.2

the requirement to serve the award forthwith, the Adjoining Owner(s) surveyor can in my opinion serve the awards on both the Building and Adjoining Owner(s) with a copy to the Building Owner(s) surveyor. The Adjoining Owner(s) Surveyor is simply adopting the same approach as the Third Surveyor would when issuing an award and thus ensuring that the 14 day appeal period commences on the same day.

The service of the award must include a clear explanation of the owner(s) rights under section 10(17) to appeal within 14 days. This commences 2 days after the documents have been consigned to the post[312] and not when it is received. On a final point the surveyor(s) must not withhold service of the award for any reason including non-payment of their fees because the liability to pay costs will not arise until the award has been served and the 14 days has expired.

12.17 Service of the Third Surveyors award

s.10(15)(a)&(b)

(15) Where an award is made by the third surveyor—

    (a)   he shall, after payment of the costs of the award, serve it forthwith on the parties or their appointed surveyors; and

    (b)   if it is served on their appointed surveyors, they shall serve it forthwith on the parties.

EXPLANATION

The Third Surveyor is the only surveyor entitled to request payment of his costs prior to the service of the award and many do so. Indeed, there are a number of eminent surveyor(s) who seem to take great pleasure

---

[312]   CPR Part 6 Service of Documents r.6.26

proclaiming that they have a substantial number of awards gathering dust on their shelves, having refused to serve their award until payment has been made. In my opinion this is neither a sensible nor commercial approach. If the award is served and not appealed[313] then any sums so awarded are due for payment. If the Owner(s) fail to pay the Third Surveyor can enforce payment within the magistrate's court.[314] An Award will have no effect until it is served and whilst I can understand that a Third Surveyor would want payment without having to incur the costs of enforcing payment which are in any event recoverable that inconvenience must surely be preferable to not receiving any payment?

12.18 The awards jurisdiction

s.10(16)

(16) The award shall be conclusive and shall not except as provided by this section be questioned in any court.

EXPLANATION

This section emphasises the significance that the legislation places upon the surveyor(s) award. It matters not whether the owner(s) separately or jointly consider whether the award is unreasonable, they are bound by the award unless it is appealed[315]

12.19 Appeals Procedure

s.10(17)(a)&(b)

---

313 Chapter12 *para* 12.19
314 Chapter 19
315 Chapter 12 *para* 12.19

(17) Either of the parties to the dispute may, within the period of fourteen days beginning with the day on which an award made under this section is served on him, appeal to the county court against the award and the county court may—

(a) rescind the award or modify it in such manner as the court thinks fit; and

(b) make such order as to costs as the court thinks fit.

EXPLANATION

The 14 day period allowed for filing an appeal is not negotiable, miss it, and the owner(s) are bound by the award.[316] Therefore, time is of the essence and establishing when time *"begins to run"* is based on the principle that it is when the Award is received.[317] However, a recent decision[318] held that time began when the Award was consigned to the post, and not received. This decision was overturned in November 2012 by the court appeal so the previous procedures under CPR remain applicable.

However, there has been some confusion over the correct procedures for appealing an award[319] and it is now accepted that whilst the CPR[320] does not specifically address appeals under the Act, CPR Part 52 and the practice direction note made under that part will apply because it is a statutory appeal. It is important that the appeal is not only filed on time but also correctly, get the application wrong and the appellant may find

---

[316] Zissis v Lukomski & Carter [2006] EWCA C iv 341

[317] CPR Part 6-r.6.26

[318] Freetown Ltd **v** Assethold Ltd [2012] EWHC 1351 (QB)

[319] Zissis v Lukomski & Carter [2006] EWCA C iv 341

[320] Civil Procedure Rules 1998

themselves without sufficient time to file a revised appeal. The parties can represent themselves in an appeal but the inherent risks of doing so are plain to see.[321] The cost of appealing an award should not be unnecessarily expensive and in any event an appeal should be followed immediately with an application for a stay of proceedings to let the parties discuss and/or negotiate the issues. This will secure the right of appeal if the negotiations are unsuccessful. If the award is considered invalid, the owners can (i) do nothing, or (ii) obtain a declaration of invalidity.

The Building Owner(s) are not entitled to commence the works upon receipt of the award unless the notice period under the Act have expired and if they do so they may be exposed to a financial risk, if the award is appealed. I always advise the owner(s) to wait for the fourteen days to expire. As an alternative to appealing an award the owner(s) can if they so wish jointly agree not to be bound by the award for any aspect of the award other than any costs awarded under the Act. If the award is not appealed, any costs awarded can be enforced under section 17.

12.20 Summary

Section 10 is without doubt the most important section of the Act because it establishes the statutory regime and the surveyor(s) jurisdiction to determine a broad area of issues when dissent occurs. If consent is given, section 10 can only be invoked if damage arises.[322] The surveyor(s) must act impartially and ensure that the proposed works do not cause damage to the Adjoining Owner(s) property. The surveyor(s) should tread carefully when considering and interpreting various sections of the Act, get it wrong and the award will be deemed a nullity. A failure to apply

---

[321]   Davies & Sleep v Wise [2006] Barnet County Court

[322]   Onigbanjo, A. v Mr & Mrs Pearson [2008] The Mayors and City of London Court

the Act properly could expose the surveyor(s) to a claim for negligence. The surveyor(s) should advise the Appointing Owner(s) of their rights under the Act, particularly with regards to section 10(11) and 12(1). The surveyor(s) must bring the dispute to a conclusion with an award and the owner(s) are bound by the award unless successfully appealed within 14 days. If an award is considered invalid, the owner(s) are not entitled to use or obliged to comply with its determination. Absent of an award, any works executed are outside of the statutory regime and surveyor(s) do not have jurisdiction to serve retrospective awards[323] or deal with any matters arising out of the unlawful works.

---

[323] Chapter 12 *para* 12.12.2

Chapter 13   Section 11—Expenses

13.1 Introduction

One of the most provocative issues that the surveyor(s) are asked to decide upon is the expenses which flow from the application of the Act. Contrary to popular belief it is not necessarily the Building Owner(s) that will be exposed to costs, which is clearly evident from various sections of the Act. The parties conduct can lead to costs being awarded against the Adjoining Owner(s) where they have acted unreasonably. Furthermore, it is often the case that the surveyor(s) will have difficulty in agreeing the Adjoining Owner(s) surveyors fees and this is probably one of the most popular areas of dispute which arises from the Act.

13.2 Liability to pay

s.11(1)(2)&(3)

11 (1) Except as provided under this section expenses of work under this Act shall be defrayed by the building owner.

(2) Any dispute as to responsibility for expenses shall be settled as provided in section 10.

(3) An expense mentioned in section 1(3)(b) shall be defrayed as there mentioned.

EXPLANATION

It is generally held that the Building Owner(s) will be responsible for the costs of executing the works and *inter alia* the Adjoining Owner(s) surveyor(s) costs and disbursements. Where a dispute arises, the appointed surveyor(s) will determine the reasonableness of such costs taking into account the parties actions when apportioning liability. It is therefore important that the surveyor(s) proactively engage in discussions about the costs. Failure to participate and following service of notice[324] will entitle a surveyor[325] to act *ex parte*.

13.3 Use, defect, and repair

s.11(4)(a)&(b)

(4) Where work carried out in exercise of the right mentioned in section 2(2)(a), and the work is necessary on account of defect or want of repair of the structure or wall concerned, the expenses shall be defrayed by the building owner and the Adjoining Owner in such proportion as has regard to—

   (a) the use which the owners respectively make or may make of the structure or wall concerned; and

   (b) responsibility for the defect or want of repair concerned, if more than one owner makes use of the structure or wall concerned.

EXPLANATION

If the Building Owner(s) intend to raise a type (a) party wall which is solely for their benefit they have to accept responsibility for all the costs.

---

[324] Chapter 12, *para* 12 12.8 and 12.9
[325] Bansal v Myers [2007] Romford County Court Unreported

If at a later date the Adjoining Owner(s) decide to enclose upon or adopt the raised section of wall, the Adjoining Owner(s) become liable and must contribute towards the costs of building the wall. The Adjoining Owner(s) now become the Building Owner(s) and are required to serve notice under section 2(2)(a) of the Act, and accordingly are responsible for the costs. However, the Building Owner(s) are entitled to recover 50% of the current cost of building the wall (not the cost incurred at the time the wall was built).

If a Building Owner(s) sells their property before the Adjoining Owner(s) has adopted the wall, the new owner(s) are entitled to the financial contribution for adopting the wall. This is based on the legal principle that when the Building Owner(s) sold their property it's value was calculated as being inclusive of the wall and therefore has already been paid for it.[326]

13.4 Proportional use and costs

s.11(5)(a)&(b)

(5) Where work is carried out in exercise of the right mentioned in section 2(2)(b) the expenses shall be defrayed by the building owner and the Adjoining Owner in such proportion as has regard to—

(a) the use which the owners respectively make or may make of the structure or wall concerned; and
(b) responsibility for the defect or want of repair concerned, if more than one owner makes use of the structure or wall concerned.

---

[326] Chapter 13, *para* 13.10

EXPLANATION

When determining liability for the costs, the surveyor(s) shall have regard to the reasonableness, and the benefit that each owner will obtain from the works and/or the liability for repair in reasonable proportions as the surveyor(s) deem appropriate.

13.5 Proportional disturbance and inconvenience

s.11(6)

(6) Where the adjoining premises are laid open in exercise of the right mentioned in section 2(2)(e) a fair allowance in respect of disturbance and inconvenience shall be paid by the building owner to the Adjoining Owner or occupier.

EXPLANATION

Determining the degree of *"fair allowance"* for any inconvenience and/or disturbance [327]will be dependent on the specifics of each project. The level of compensation must be reasonable, for example if the Adjoining Owner(s) had to move out of their premises, the alternative accommodation costs together with out of pocket expenses for dining out or increased travelling costs, costs of packing and relocating furniture (if necessary) would be recoverable. It may also be reasonable to award a daily rate for the inconvenience and disturbance. The Surveyor(s) must adopt a pragmatic, impartial, and sensible approach to dealing with the issue of costs, compensation must not be punitive although given the

---

[327] Emms v Polya [1973] 227 EG 1659

recent judgement[328] the courts are now considering substantial damages for unreasonable conduct of the parties and now include harassment.

13.6 Retaining the height of the wall

s.11(7)(a)&(b)

(7) Where a building owner proposes to reduce the height of a party wall or party fence wall under section 2(2)(m) the Adjoining Owner may serve a counter notice under section 4 requiring the building owner to maintain the existing height of the wall, and in such case the Adjoining Owner shall pay to the building owner a due proportion of the cost of the wall so far as it exceeds—

(a) two metres in height; or
(b) the height currently enclosed upon the building of the Adjoining Owner.

EXPLANATION

There can be no doubt that the introduction of section 11(7) flows from the decision in Gyle-Thompson v Wall Street (Properties) Ltd[329] where it was held that there was no right under the 1939 Act to reduce the height of the party wall or party fence wall. In Gyle-Thompson, the surveyor(s) had unlawfully authorised such works, although was complicated further because there were procedural irregularities which invalidated the award in any event. Notwithstanding, the introduction of this section of the Act does not automatically grant the Building Owner(s) the right

---

[328] Jones & Lovegrove v Ruth & Ruth [2012} EWHC 1538 and in the Court of Appeal [2011]

[329] Gyle-Thompson v Wall Street (Properties) Ltd 1 WLR 123 [1974] 1 ALL ER 295

to reduce the height of the wall because the Adjoining Owner(s) have certain rights[330] and benefits over the wall and if they can demonstrate that the height should be retained they could successfully prevent these alterations.

13.7 Cash Settlement

s.11(8)

(8) Where the building owner is required to make good damage under this Act the Adjoining Owner has a right to require that the expenses of such making good be determined in accordance with section 10 and paid to him in lieu of the carrying out of work to make the damage good.

EXPLANATION

In my opinion settling the matter with a cash payment is the most effective way of bringing a claim to a natural conclusion. The payment will be on a full and final settlement and therefore eliminates any further liability. The Adjoining Owner(s) are not obliged to spend the cash on the works, and when accepting a cash settlement will be responsible for the performance of their contractors when executing those works. In the first instance this may not be the most economical approach for a commercial developer who could source the works at a more commercial rate but it does give finality and that in the long term could be the most economical approach.

---

[330] Chapter 11, *para* 11.2

13.8 Adjoining Owners liability to costs

s.11(9)(a)&(b)

(9) Where—

(a) works are carried out, and
(b) some of the works are carried out at the request of the Adjoining Owner or in pursuance of a requirement made by him,

he shall defray the expenses of carrying out the works requested or required by him.

EXPLANATION

The Adjoining Owner(s) have the right to request the Building Owner(s) carry out certain works. In these circumstances it is only correct that the Adjoining Owner(s) are responsible for the reasonable costs of those works. However, the Building Owner(s) cannot see this as an opportunity to recover some of their earlier costs by charging inflated rates. The surveyor(s) will determine the reasonableness of any costs and should obtain estimates before awarding the works and/or liabilities for costs.

13.9 Special Foundations with Consent

s.11(10)(a)&(b)

(10) Where—

(a) consent in writing has been given to the construction of special foundations on land of an Adjoining Owner; and

(b) the Adjoining Owner erects any building or structure and its cost is found to be increased by reason of the existence of the said foundations,

The owner of the building to which the said foundations belong shall, on receiving an account with any necessary invoices and other supporting documents within the period of two months beginning with the day of the completion of the work by the Adjoining Owner, repay to the Adjoining Owner so much of the cost as is due to the existence of the said foundations.

EXPLANATION

In my opinion, this is another reason why foundations (special or otherwise) should never be projected onto an Adjoining Owners properties. It opens too may avenues for future disputes and could have an adverse effect on the capital value of the parties respective properties. The award always remains with the property and any benefits or liabilities will transfer to future owner(s), careful consideration of the wording *"the said foundations belong"* is therefore necessary. The surveyor(s) have a duty to advise the owner(s) of the potential adverse consequences of giving consent.

13.10 Benefit in Kind

s.11(11)

(11) Where use is subsequently made by the Adjoining Owner of work carried out solely at the expense of the building owner the Adjoining Owner shall pay a due proportion of the expenses incurred by the building owner in carrying out that work; and for this purpose he shall be taken to have incurred expenses calculated by reference to

what the cost of the work would be if it were carried out at the time when that subsequent use is made.

EXPLANATION

If the Building Owner(s) undertakes work purely for their benefit and the Adjoining Owner(s) decides at a later date to use the wall, it is only correct that the Adjoining Owner(s) contributes to the costs of those works.[331] This section to a certain extent reinforces the principles discussed *supra* and maintains the principle of fairness.

13.11 Summary

Section 11 is really all about fairness and ensuring that the owner(s) pay an appropriate contribution when use is made of the structure. The benefit and/or liability remains with the property, not the owner(s), and therefore the surveyor(s) have a duty of care to advise the Owner(s) of their obligation to inform prospective purchasers when passing on any liability or benefit upon sale of the property. The liabilities that may flow from projecting a foundation create an unknown future liability and may have implication when selling the property.

---

[331] Chapter 13, *para* 13.3

Chapter 14 Section 12—Security of Expenses

14.1 Introduction

This section will protect an owner from a loss in the event that the owner(s) are unable to satisfy any financial obligations arising from the works. This becomes particularly more relevant and foreseeable when the Adjoining Owner(s) property has been laid open or rights of access are being exercised.

14.2 Adjoining Owners Security

s.12(1)

12(1)   An Adjoining Owner may serve a notice requiring the building owner before he begins any work in the exercise of the rights conferred by this Act to give such security as may be agreed between the owners or in the event of dispute determined in accordance with section 10.

EXPLANATION

The right to serve notice requesting security is explicit, the Adjoining Owner(s) *"may"* serve a notice and it is therefore their decision. The Appointed Surveyor(s) jurisdiction only arises, if the owner(s) cannot agree on the amount of security. Obviously the request for security will create a financial burden on the Building Owner(s) but that is irrelevant.

Given the recent decision in some cases[332] the surveyor(s) must apply the principle of *"reasonably foreseeable"* when considering the level of security. It will therefore be project specific and should include all reasonably foreseeable costs. The security can be provided in a variety of forms such as cash deposited in an account, an insurance policy in the owner(s) names, or a debenture or other form of security as may reasonably be determined. However, the surveyor(s) have a statutory obligation to advise the owner(s) of their rights.

The surveyor(s) who ignore this section and their obligation to advise the owner(s) of their rights do so at their peril. The following narrative is a true account of a party wall matter which illustrates the importance of section 12(1).

An Agreed Surveyor having been validly appointed had disastrous consequences when the execution of the works caused substantial structural damage to the Adjoining Owner(s) property. Whilst the Agreed Surveyor awarded costs against the Building Owners (company A) of approximately £30,000 exclusive of VAT. Company A did not have insurance and subsequently sold the site to Company B[333] who continued with the development. Company 'A' went into liquidation leaving the Adjoining Owner(s) to claim on his buildings policy. The Adjoining Owner(s) insurers reluctantly accepted liability, but took legal advice. I was instructed to forensically examine the procedures and it became clear that the Agreed Surveyor had failed to advise the Adjoining Owner(s) that they were entitled to request security of expenses prior to commencement of the works. A claim was made against the Agreed Surveyor's insurers who settled the claim in full. This case demonstrates how precarious the party wall surveyor(s) position is and even more so

---

[332] Jones & Lovegrove v Ruth & Ruth [2012} EWHC 1538 and in the Court of Appeal [2011]

[333] The directors of Company A also owned company B

when acting as an Agreed Surveyor. I believe the Agreed Surveyor was liable because he failed to discharge his duty of care. When accepting an appointment, the surveyor(s) must advise the owners of their rights under the Act. The Agreed Surveyor could have avoided any allegation of negligence by simply advising the Adjoining Owner(s) of their right under section 12(1). If the Adjoining Owner(s) had decided not to request any security, the Agreed Surveyor would not have been held responsible because he had discharged his duty of care.

14.3 Building owner's security

s.12(2)(a)&(b)

(2) Where—

(a) in the exercise of the rights conferred by this Act an Adjoining Owner requires the building owner to carry out any work the expenses of which are to be defrayed in whole or in part by the Adjoining Owner; or

(b) an Adjoining Owner serves a notice on the building owner under subsection (1),

the building owner may before beginning the work to which the requirement or notice relates serve a notice on the Adjoining Owner requiring him to give such security as may be agreed between the owners or in the event of dispute determined in accordance with section 10.

EXPLANATION

If the Adjoining Owner(s) serves a notice requesting the Building Owner(s) do certain works which are for the benefit of the Adjoining Owner(s), then all of the costs fall upon the Adjoining Owner(s) and quite rightly so. There is no restriction on the type of works that can be requested and accordingly the Building Owner(s) are equally entitled to request security of expenses to ensure that payment is available. The same principles with regards to security of expenses apply.

The role of the Surveyor(s) is (i) to ensure that the Adjoining Owner(s) do not get overcharged for the works and (ii) that the Building Owner(s) are paid for those works. The parties may agree[334] that the Building Owner(s) will pay for the costs of the works in return for some other consideration such as a right of access for works which are not available under the Act. In certain circumstances a bartering position between the owner(s) can arise, but this is outside the surveyor(s) jurisdiction, unless the parties expressly and independently instruct them to participate.

14.4 Adjoining Owners Request for building works

s.(12)(3)(a)&9(b)

(3)   If within the period of one month beginning with—

(a)   the day on which a notice is served under subsection (2); or
(b)   in the event of dispute, the date of the determination by the surveyor or surveyors,

the Adjoining Owner does not comply with the notice or the determination, the requirement or notice by him to which the building owner's notice under that subsection relates shall cease to have effect.

---

[334]   Chapter 1, *para* 1.3

EXPLANATION

This is further evidence that the Act seeks to eliminate any delays by incorporating a notice period on the principle that the Act is therefore a double edged sword and quite rightly so.

14.5 Summary

On the face of it this is a short but important section designed to prevent the Owner(s) suffering a loss from either the Building Owner(s) or Adjoining Owner(s) requests. The degree of reasonable security will be determined on the merits of the project. The surveyor(s) have a duty *inter alia* to advise the owner(s) of their statutory rights. A failure to do so could place a liability upon the surveyor(s). The award should include sufficient security as is reasonably foreseeable to allow the satisfactory and proper completion of the works and/or where an owner is entitled to claim compensation. The surveyor(s) will include within the award the appropriate security and if the Owner(s) do not comply with the award, the aggrieved party can at common law enforce the award.

Chapter 15   Section 13—Expenses

15.1 Introduction

Where there is a requirement to provide security of expenses or contribute towards the cost of certain aspects of the works, it is only right that the Act incorporates a means for recovery of such expenses.

15.2 Claiming expenses for works

s.13(1)(a)&(b)

13(1)   Within the period of two months beginning with the day of the completion of any work executed by a building owner of which the expenses are to be wholly or partially defrayed by an Adjoining Owner in accordance with section 11 the building owner shall serve on the Adjoining Owner an account in writing showing—

(a)   particulars and expenses of the work; and

(b)   any deductions to which the Adjoining Owner or any other person is entitled in respect of old materials or otherwise;

and in preparing the account the works shall be estimated and valued at fair average rates and prices according to the nature of the work, the locality and the cost of labour and materials prevailing at the time when the work is executed.

EXPLANATION

The same principles regarding finality of notice periods apply miss the time frame and the Building Owner(s) will lose the right to recover any costs incurred. If the account is challenged section 10 shall apply. The surveyor(s) must demonstrate a reasonable and pragmatic approach when determining the reasonable costs and include the grounds for reaching the decision within the Award.[335]

15.3 Challenging reasonableness of expenses

s.13(2)&(3)

(2)   Within the period of one month beginning with the day of service of the said account the Adjoining Owner may serve on the building owner a notice stating any objection he may have thereto and thereupon a dispute shall be deemed to have arisen between the parties.

(3)   If within that period of one month the Adjoining Owner does not serve notice under subsection (2) he shall be deemed to have no objection to the account.

EXPLANATION

The Adjoining Owner(s) must comply with this time frame or loose the right to challenge the costs. If the Adjoining Owner(s) are waiting on information to support their objection they should notify the Building Owner(s) and/or the surveyor(s) and in such circumstances it would be unreasonable not to allow an extension of time.

---

[335]   Davies & Sleep v Wise [2006] Barnet County Court

15.4 Summary

If the owner(s) cannot resolve their differences the matter shall be settled by the appointed surveyor(s) adopting the same provisions under section 10 to ensure that the various owner(s) pay and/or receive their legitimate expenses that have reasonably been incurred. The right for submitting and/or challenging any costs will expire when the time periods *supra* have passed.

Chapter 16   Adjoining Owners account

16.1 Introduction

This section establishes the Adjoining Owner(s) obligation to pay any costs incurred and is relatively straight forward to interpret and apply.

16.2 Adjoining Owners liabilities

Section 14—

14(1)   All expenses to be defrayed by an Adjoining Owner in accordance with an account served under section 13 shall be paid by the Adjoining Owner.

Until the Adjoining Owner pays to the building owner such expenses as aforesaid the property in any works executed under this Act to which the expenses relate shall be vested solely in the building owner.

16.3 Explanation

If the Adjoining Owner(s) fail to settle any accounts under section 13, the Building Owner(s) can ask the surveyor(s) including the Third Surveyor under[336] to serve an award and then recover payment through the magistrate's court as a civil debt.[337]

---

[336]   Chapter 12 *para* 12.13
[337]   Chapter 19 *para* 19.2

15.4 Summary

The principle of retaining title to the goods is of little or no value to the Building Owner(s) when in reality he would not go back into the property and pull down or remove parts of the structure (even if he could obtain lawful access) because this only increases his loss[338]

---

[338] Time incurred in demolishing

Chapter 17   Section 15—Miscellaneous (service of notices etc)

17.1 Introduction

Earlier in the book I explained that relationships between neighbours may be less than friendly and the Adjoining Owner(s) may attempt to prevent the works from proceeding by refusing to accept or acknowledge service of the notice(s). This section helpfully sets out the various methods of validly serving the notice and invoking the statutory regime when the Adjoining Owner(s) are non-responsive. However, if the Building Owner(s) deviate away from the prescribed format, the notice(s) may not be deemed to have been served and anything done thereafter would be invalid.

17.2 Service

s.15(1)(a)(b)&(c)

15(1)   A notice or other document required or authorised to be served under this Act may be served on a person—

    (a)   by delivering it to him in person;

    (b)   by sending it by post to him at his usual or last known residence or place of business in the United Kingdom; or

    (c)   in the case of a body corporate, by delivering it to the secretary or clerk of that body corporate at that office.

EXPLANATION

It is generally held that the Civil Procedure Rules do not apply because this is statute rather than civil litigation, which may seem a contradiction when debts under section 17 are recoverable summarily as a civil debt. However, in my opinion there is evidence to support the principle that they apply. Until recently and in the absence of any legal authority I have adopted the principles set out within the Civil Procedure Rules[339] to determine the time frame for deeming service of documents to have occurred by adding 48 hours to the 14 days as set out under the Act. However, a recent case changed this approach[340] when an appeal[341] was struck out on the basis that it was filed out of time because the 14 day statutory period had expired before the appeal had been filed.[342] The decision was appealed on the basis that the 14 day period ran from the day it was received and not the day that it was posted. Mr Recorder Hochhauser QC relied on the earlier legal decision[343] and held that the date of service was not the date on which the recipient received the documents, but the date on which the documents were posted, which is clearly contrary to CPR Part 6 R.6.26 although this decision has now been set aside by the court of appeal and CPR Part 6 applies.

Accordingly, for a party to successfully prevent an appeal being struck out on the basis that it is out of time, they will have to demonstrate certainty of the date on which the document was consigned to the post to ensure that the appeal is within time. I would not advise using recorded delivery because if the document is not signed for it may not

---

[339] Part 6, r 6.26

[340] CPR Part 6 Service of Documents r.6.26

[341] Chapter 12 *para* 12.19

[342] Zissis v Lukomski & Carter [2006] EWCA C iv 341

[343] CA Webber (Transport) Ltd v Railtrack Plc [2003] EWCA Civ 1167

been delivered whereas obtaining a certificate of posting starts the clock ticking.

The method of service determined by this section is neither mandatory or exhaustive, as suggested[344] the owner(s) are entitled to reach an agreement outside of the Act's procedures and in regard to service and/or receipt of notices invariably do so when they appoint their surveyor.[345] The letters of appointment will invariably use words such as *"In the event of dissent we will appoint and/or authorise our surveyor Mr X to sign, serve, and/or receive notices on our behalf"*. This clearly supersedes the statutory provisions as set out supra and the surveyor(s) could agree that service by email or fax is acceptable.

17.3 Adjoining Owner(s) identity

s.15(2)(a)&(b)

(2)   In the case of a notice or other document required or authorised to be served under this Act on a person as owner of premises, it may alternatively be served by—

(a)   addressing it "the owner" of the premises (naming them), and

(b)   delivering it to a person on the premises or, if no person to whom it can be delivered is found there, fixing it to a conspicuous part of the premises.

---

[344]   See Chapter 1, *para* 1.3
[345]   Chapter 23

EXPLANATION

It is not always possible to obtain the names of the Adjoining Owner(s)/ occupier(s) therefore, whilst the Building Owner(s) names must be included on the notices, there is no requirement to include the Adjoining Owner(s) or occupiers names, simply addressing the notices to the *"owner(s)Occupiers"* satisfies the provisions under the Act.

17.4 Summary

This section provides alternative titles methods of service of notices and/ or documents, get the process or timing wrong and everything thereafter may be deemed invalid. The most effective method of service is to use Royal Mail and obtain a certificate of posting, this will be sufficient to demonstrate when time begins.

Chapter 18   Section 16—Offences

18.1 Introduction

This is another section that is often overlooked by the surveyor(s) and do not advise the owner(s) or occupier(s) of the consequences of refusing or allowing a person to do anything which they are entitled to do under the Act. The Act clearly has teeth and if adopted properly where an obstruction occurs can ensure compliance and/or can impose significant penalties on the offending owner(s)/occupier(s).

18.2 Obstruction

s.16(1)(a)&(b)

16(1)   If—

(a)   an occupier of land or premises refused to permit a person to do anything which he is entitled to do with regard to the land or premises under section 8(1) or (5); and

(b)   the occupier knows or has reasonable cause to believe that the person is so entitled,

the occupier is guilt of an offence.

EXPLANATION

In one very frustrating party wall project the Building Owner(s) were arrested for public order offences following threats of violence. In another case an injunction was obtained and when both Building Owner(s) breached the injunction on two separate occasions, an application for committal[346] was made by the Adjoining Owner(s). Whilst this was an unusual and thankfully rare occurrence, it demonstrates that not all owner(s) will act rationally and/or reasonably.

18.3 Hindrance

s.16(2)(a)&(b)

(2) If—

    (a)   a person hinders or obstructs a person in attempting to do anything which he is entitled to do with regard to land or premises under section 8(1) or (5); and

    (b)   the first-mentioned person is guilty of an offence.

EXPLANATION

The surveyor(s) owe a duty of care to advise the owner(s) of the consequences of hindering the lawful activities of any person. Sub-section (b) would appear to remove any defence to the charge. The owner(s) must be advised of the consequences of any such actions.

---

[346] Apply for a custodial sentence

18.4 Conviction

s.16(3)

(3)   A person guilty of an offence under subsection (1) or (2) is liable on summary conviction to a fine of an amount not exceeding level 3 on the standard scale.

EXPLANATION

I have no knowledge or experience of any person being prosecuted under section 16 however if they are, it would be heard in the Magistrates Court and on summary conviction liable to a fine which should not exceed level 3 on the standard scale which is currently £1,000.00.

18.5 Summary

This section reinforces the importance the Act places upon the owner(s) obligations to ensure that matters proceed without unreasonable interference, if the owner(s) obstruct or hinder the work, they can be prosecuted.

Chapter 19　Section 17—Recovery of Expenses

19.1 Introduction

This section sets out the correct procedures for the recovery of any sums so awarded. This section maintains the importance of the Act by ensuring that the owner(s) can recover their costs when seeking payment within the magistrate's court which has significant benefits than the county court system.

19.2 Magistrates Court

s.17

17　Any sum payable in pursuance of this Act (otherwise than by way of a fine) shall be recoverable summarily as a civil debt.

EXPLANATION

The Act clearly anticipated situations where an owner might fail to pay the sum so awarded and helpfully section 17 allows any sum payable to be recovered summarily as a civil debt. The definition of a civil debt is found under chapter 43, section 150(1) of the Magistrates Court Act 1980. Accordingly, it is open for any party under section 17 to serve a complaint under section 58 of the Magistrates Court Act 1980 which is now helpfully referenced within the 2011 edition of the Stones Justices

Manual. In my opinion the correct process to enforce payment is to adopt The Magistrates Court Act 1980.

19.2.1   The Procedure

Legal advice should be obtained before commencing any litigation but as a general principal I would suggest that the owner(s) should serve a pre-action letter explaining the intention to commence litigation and provide seven days for payment to be made. The letter should clearly set out the remedy (payment of sums awarded) and what they are required to do to avoid litigation. The liability for further costs and/or interest should also be included in the pre-action letter. Service of all correspondence should be properly recorded[347] and served.

If the pre-action letter does not achieve a positive response the claimant must first serve a written complaint to the Justices' Clerk of the local Magistrates Court. The Magistrates Court (Forms) Rules 1981 suggest either Form 98 or 104; the technically correct version is the latter. Using the prescribed form will eliminate any mistakes which may be used as a technicality by the defendants to prevent the complaint from being heard. The complaint should include a statement that it is made under section 17 of *The Party Wall etc. Act 1996* and most certainly should include the parties' full names and addresses and identify them as either the defendant or claimant with the claimant's contact telephone number. The complaint should have an appended bundle which must include *inter alia* (i) all notices and letters of appointment (ii) a signed copy of the award (iii) the pre-action letters requesting payment, (iv) and all correspondence that advises the defendants of the consequences should they continue to ignore the award and fail to pay the sums so awarded, (v) proof of posting, (vi) Copies of Fee accounts, (vii) a schedule of the costs.

---

[347]   Chapter 17 *para* 17.2

19.2.2　Costs

The issue of cost for recovering a debt is obviously paramount and in such circumstances may be substantially greater than the amount being sought. It would be very perverse if the surveyor(s) or owner(s) had to pay more in legal costs than the debt was worth. To be able to recover costs of the application, the award should include a clear reference to "other contingencies".[348] The claimant can recover their costs for preparing the case, attendance at court, solicitors, and of course counsels fees. It would also be wise to include the total amount that the claimant seeks to recover, supported with a breakdown of how those costs have been calculated and an estimate for any further costs.

The magistrates' court currently charge £200 (per defendant) for processing the complaint, irrespective of the amount being recovered. The magistrates' court will then prepare the summons for the claimants to serve upon the defendants. The case will be heard relatively quickly (certainly substantially quicker than the county court). The claimants must attend and will be required to give evidence under Oath. However, if the defendant fails to attend the matter can still proceed in their absence. The Court will make the relevant order and will consider any costs on the principle that they are just and reasonable under section 64(1) of the Magistrates' Court Act 1980. These will be added to the sum stated in the complaint. There are time limits within which a claimant must commence the action, (governed by the Limitation Act 1980) enforcement of a civil debt must be commenced within six months of the date that the debt falls due which is generally the date of the award, or if an invoice has been rendered. The ability to recover these costs within the Magistrate's Court is infinitely more likely than the County

---

[348]　Chapter 23, *para* 23.7 & 23.8

Court. One final benefit to the surveyor is the right to have the case filed with their local magistrate's court.

19.2.3   Deed of Assignment

The Adjoining Owner(s) are unlikely to want to become involved litigation to obtain payment of their surveyor's' fees, because in most circumstances surveyor(s) will tell their appointing owner(s) that the Building Owner(s) will pay them. In these situations the Adjoining Owner(s) surveyor can have a deed of assignment prepared that will allow them to step into the shoes of the Adjoining Owner(s) and commence litigation to recover any sums awarded under the Act.

19.3 Summary

This is a very powerful section because it provides a very quick and cost effective approach for achieving payment under the Act. I would not encourage any other method because the sums awarded under the Act are explicitly referred to as a civil debt and I believe that they should be recovered as such. The Magistrate's Court process is quicker and allows a greater opportunity to recover all of the costs involved.

Chapter 20 Section 18—Exclusions

20.1 Introduction

This section identifies the parties that are excluded from compliance with the statutory regime.

20.2 Barrister's exclusion

s.18(1)(a)(b)(c)&(d) and (2)

18(1)   This Act shall not apply to land which is situated in inner London and in which there is an interest belonging to—

    (a)   the Honourable Society of the Inner Temple,
    (b)   the Honourable Society of the Middle Temple.
    (c)   the Honourable Society of Lincoln's Inn, or
    (d)   the Honourable Society of Gray's Inn.

(2)   The reference in subsection (1) to inner London is to Greater London other than the outer London Boroughs.

EXPLANATION

I am not quite sure why the Honourable Society of the Inner and Middle temples or Society of Lincoln's and Grey's Inn are exempt when Her Majesty is not? Given that the Act provides benefits and remedies to property owner(s) one would have thought that these august societies would have wanted to embrace the benefits and protection the Act provides.

20.3 Summary

This section is clear and requires no further explanation other than to invite these bodies to perhaps explain why they were excluded.

Chapter 21　Section 19—Inclusions

21.1 Introduction

This section demonstrates that even the most revered and highest in the land are required to comply with the Act.

21.2 Queen Elizabeth II

s.19)(1)(a)(b)&(c) and (2)(a)&(b)

19(1)　This Act shall apply to land in which there is—

    (a)　an interest belonging to Her Majesty in right of the Crown,

    (b)　an interest belonging to a government department, or

    (c)　an interest held in trust for her Majesty for the purposes of any such department.

EXPLANATION

Given that the Act is applicable to her Majesty Queen Elizabeth II and the properties related to governmental departments or an interest held in trust for her Majesty, makes the exclusions under section 18 even more peculiar. However, I do find it amusing to think that one day a surveyor might actually serve notice upon her Majesty Queen Elizabeth II or indeed be appointed under section 10(4) on her behalf.

21.3 Duchy of Lancaster and Cornwall

(2) This Act shall apply to—

    (a) land which is vested in, but not occupied by, Her Majesty in right of the Duchy of Lancaster;

    (b) land which is vested in, but not occupied by, the possessor for the time being of the Duchy of Cornwall.

EXPLANATION

The same observations under section 19(1) apply.

21.4 Summary

It is not clear why there is a separate section for Her Majesty, given that she is clearly considered to be an owner under the Act, and would be subjected to the statutory regime in the same manner as everyone else. However, this section clearly reinforces the principles that the Act applies to almost everyone.

Chapter 22   Basements

22.1 Introduction

In recent years the construction industry has experienced an unprecedented explosion in basement extensions which is now on par (in volume) with loft conversions. Advances in damp proofing and innovative engineering designs are creating substantial subterranean developments. However, the definition of special foundations can determine whether the basement can be constructed. In their desire to satisfy the Building Owner(s) demands, the Adjoining Owner(s) rights are regularly compromised, ignored, and/or abused because of the confusion surrounding the vertical elements of the basement construction.

22.2 Wall or Foundation

The right to raise the party wall downwards is a recent issue which has caused considerable debate and disparity within the party wall community. It is held by some that the construction of a basement wall is the opposite to raising a party wall upwards and therefore allowable[349] if the vertical section of the basement is a wall and not a special foundation. If this interpretation is correct, the Building Owner(s) can avoid the need for written consent for special foundations and use whatever materials they choose such as reinforced concrete to construct the basement walls,

---

[349]   Chapter 4, *para* 4.3.1

because it is defined as an extension of the party wall and not a special foundation.

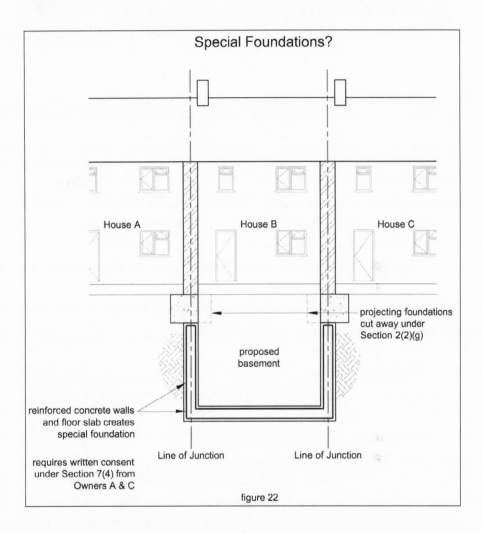

figure 22

Alternatively, some surveyor(s) believe the structural function of the wall is a method of underpinning and allowable under section 2. In my opinion, the basement wall cannot be classified as having a single function. It is by definition multi-functional acting as underpinning[350] to the wall above, a foundation which replaces the natural right of support to the Adjoining Owner(s) soil, a wall that forms the habitable environment of the Basement and special foundations which requires consent. It is not a party fence wall and most certainly is not built against an Adjoining Owner(s) structure and therefore cannot be a type (b) party wall. The vertical elements of the basement are either an extension to the existing type (a) party wall or a new type (a) party wall which will requires notice and the Adjoining Owners(s) consent because it extends across the boundary.[351]

I would point out that the property owner(s) share a natural right of support from neighbouring owner(s) land.[352] When the Building Owner(s) decide to construct a basement they will interfere with and/or disturb the natural support. The principal held in Selby v Whitbread established the Building Owner(s) rights to interfere with a right of support insofar as they are able to provide and maintain an alternative method of support. The basement wall is an alternative means of support designed to resist the lateral forces created by the Adjoining Owner(s) soil and must by definition be a foundation, which if incorporating reinforcing is a special foundation requiring the Adjoining Owner(s) written consent.

22.3 Linkage

In my opinion the reinforcement is the key to determining the function of the elements of the basement and whether written consent for the special foundations is required. If the basement wall is linked to the basement floor slab/raft they cannot be treated as independent structural elements and must because of the inclusion of an assemblage of beams

---

[350] Absent of any subsidence.
[351] Chapter 3, *para* 3.3
[352] Chapter 11, *para* 11.5

and/or create a special foundation irrespective of whether one element is vertical and the other is horizontal. The Act does not distinguish between vertical and horizontal elements when considering a party structure and I see no reason to depart from applying the same accepted principle for special foundations. In my opinion the whole basement construction must therefore be considered a special foundation, requiring written consent for those elements which are positioned across the line of junction.

22.4 Summary

I accept this view is contentious and some surveyor(s) will suggest that the wall should be considered separately, but for the reasons above and with the intention to provoke healthy discussion I do not think it is, and until I am presented with a legal precedent or a persuasive argument to the contrary will approach basements on this basis.

Chapter 23 Specimen Documents

23.1 Proposed Letter of Surveyors Appointment

Address

11th April 2011

Addressee

Dear **[Insert Appointed Surveyors Name]**,

Re: Party Wall etc. Act 1996 56 & 58 Tryfan Close Redbridge IG4 5JY

We **[Insert Appointing Owners Full Names]** appoint **[Insert Appointed Surveyors Name and address]** to sign, serve, and receive all and any notices in relation to the party wall procedures in accordance with s.10(1)(a) or s.10(1)(b) **[delete as appropriate]** of the Act in connection with this proposed development and make any necessary appointments on our behalf, that are relevant and subject to notification under the Party Wall etc Act 1996.

Yours sincerely,

. . . .

Name   Name

Date   Date

23.2 Section 1 Line of Junction

Party Wall etc. Act 1996

SECTION 1 LINE OF JUNCTION NOTICE

To:
Of:

As Adjoining Owner/s under the Act of the premises known as:

We:
Of:

As Building Owner/s under the Act of:

Which adjoins your premises:

HEREBY SERVE YOU WITH NOTICE UNDER THAT UNDER

section 1(2)
section 1 (5)

That it is intended to build on the line of junction of the said properties a wall wholly on our land.

section 1(6)

That it is intended to place projecting footings and foundations on your land at our expense

section 7(4)

Delete any of the sections that are not applicable

Following your written consent, it is proposed to use special foundations as detailed in the accompanying drawings listed her with:

It is intended to commence works after one month or earlier by agreement. In the event of a dispute under section 1(8), section 10 of the Act requires that both parties should concur in the appointment of a Surveyor, or should each appoint one Surveyor and in those circumstances I/We would appoint as my/our Surveyor: **[insert surveyors name]**.

Of: **[Insert Surveyors Address]**

SIGNED:

Authorised to sign on behalf of (Building Owner/s)

DATE: Date of Posting

22.3 Party Structure Notice

Party Wall etc. Act 1996

SECTION 2 PARTY STRUCTURE NOTICE

To:
Of:

As Adjoining Owner/s under the Act of the premises known as:

We:
Of:

As owner of:

Which adjoins your premises known as:

HEREBY SERVE YOU WITH NOTICE

THAT IN ACCORDANCE WITH MY RIGHTS under Section 2 Subsection (2) **[insert sub-sections]** and with reference to the PARTY STRUCTURE/PARTY WALL separating the above premises, it is intended to carry out the works detailed below, after the expiration of **two months** from service of this Notice and drawing Numbers:—**[insert drawing titles]**.

The proposed works are:

[Enter description of works]

It is intended to commence works on expiry of the two months or earlier by agreement.

If you do not consent to the works within 14 days a dispute will be deemed to have arisen. In this case s.10(1)(a) of the Act allows the owners to jointly agree in the appointment of an agreed Surveyor or under s.10(1)(b) each owner should appoint one Surveyor and in those circumstances I/We would appoint: **[insert Building Owners name and address]**

SIGNED:

Authorised to sign on behalf of **[insert building owner(s) name]** (Building Owner)

DATE:

23.4 Notices—Acknowledgement of Party Structure Notice

Party Wall etc. Act 1996

ACKNOWLEDGEMENT OF PARTY STRUCTURE NOTICE

I

Of:

As Adjoining Owner/s under the Act of the premises known as:

Having received the Notice served by: Mr & Mrs Adamson

Of:

In respect of:

Which adjoins my/our premises, and in relation to the works proposed under 2 subsection (2), paragraphs: [insert appropriate sub-sections]

Hereby CONSENT to the proposed works

Or

Hereby DISSENT from the above works and a dispute having arisen, concur with the appointment of **[insert building owner(s) surveyors name and address]** as An AGREED SURVEYOR.

OR IN THE ALTERNATIVE /I Appoint:

Of:

SIGNED:

Authorised to sign on behalf of **[insert Adjoining Owners name]**

DATE:

23.5 3m/6m Notice

Party Wall Etc. Act 1996

NOTICE UNDER SECTION 6(1) OR (2) THREE METRE/SIX METRE NOTICE (delete as appropriate)

To:
Of:

As the Adjoining Owner/s under the Act of the premises known as:

We:
Of:

As building Owner/s under the Act of:

Which adjoins your premises

HEREBY SERVE YOU WITH NOTICE THAT IN ACCORDANCE WITH MY/OUR RIGHTS

Under section 6 (1) or (2) **(delete as appropriate)** it is intended to excavate and/or build within 3/6 metres of your building and to a lower level than the bottom of your foundations, by carrying out the works detailed below, after the expiration of one month from the service of this Notice or earlier by agreement.

Or

IT IS/IS NOT PROPOSED TO UNDERPIN OR OTHERWISE STRENGTHEN IN ORDER TO SAFEGUARD THE FOUNDATIONS OF YOUR BUILDING

The accompanying plans and section show the site and the excavation depth proposed.

The intended works are: **[insert description]**

To excavate foundations to a depth of [enter description] below ground level, and to a greater depth if determined by Local Authority building. **[insert drawing numbers]**

It is intended to commence works when Notice has run or earlier by agreement. Under s.6(7), if you do not consent to the works within 14 days a dispute is deemed to have arisen. In this case s.10(1)(a) of the Act allows the owner(s) to agree the appointment of an Agreed Surveyor or if they cannot agree s.10(1)(b) each owner should appoint one Surveyor and in those circumstances I/We would appoint: **[insert Building Owner(s) surveyors name and address]**.

Of: **[insert Building Owner(s) surveyors address]**.

SIGNED:
Authorised to sign on behalf of **[insert Building Owners names]** (Building Owner/s)

DATED:

23.6 Acknowledgement of 3m/6m Notice

Party Wall etc. Act 1996

ACKNOWLEDGEMENT OF THREE/SIX METRE NOTICE

We:
Of:

As Adjoining Owner/s under the Act of the premises known as:

Having received the Notice served by:

Of:
In respect of:

Which adjoins my/our premises:

Hereby CONSENT to the proposed works

Or

Require you to safeguard or underpin the foundations of my/our building

Or

Dispute to necessity for underpinning or strengthening the foundations of my/our building.

Hereby DISSENT from the above works and a dispute having arisen, concur in the appointment of **[Insert building owners surveyors name and address]** as An AGREED SURVEYOR.

OR IN THE ALTERNATIVE /We Appoint:

Of:

SIGNED:

Authorised to sign on behalf of **[insert Adjoining Owner(s) names]** (Adjoining Owner/s)

DATE:

23.7 Draft Award Agreed Surveyor

AN AWARD under the provisions
Of the PARTY WALL etc. ACT,
1996 to be served on the
Appointing Owners under Section 10(14)

WHEREAS **[insert Building Owner(s) name(s)]** (hereinafter referred to as the Building Owner) of **[insert Building Owner(s) address]** freehold owners within the meaning of the said Act of the premises known as **[insert address of property where works will be undertaken]** did on the **[insert date of notice(s)]** serve upon **[insert Adjoining Owners name(s)]** (hereinafter referred to as the Adjoining Owner) freehold owner within the meaning of the Act of the adjoining premises known as **[insert address of Adjoining Owner(s)]**, Notice of their intention to exercise the rights given to them by the Party Wall etc Act 1996 **[insert details of notices served]**

AND WHEREAS the Building and Adjoining Owner's have appointed **[insert name and address of Agreed Surveyor]** to act as the **Agreed Surveyor** in accordance with Section 10(1)(a).

NOW I, being the **Agreed Surveyor** so appointed, having inspected the said premises DO HEREBY AWARD AND DETERMINE as follows:—

1. (a) That the wall separating the building owners and adjoining owners premises is deemed to be a party wall within the meaning of the Act.

    (b) That the Adjoining Owners' building stands close to the Building Owners premises within the meaning of the Act.

(c)   That the Schedule of Conditions dated **[insert date if applicable]** attached hereto and signed by me the said agreed Surveyor forms part of this Award.

(d)   That the said Party Wall as described in the attached Schedule of Condition is sufficient for the present purposes of the Adjoining Owner.

(e)   That Drawings Nos. **[insert drawing details]** attached hereto and any others which may become relevant and signed by me the Agreed Surveyor form part of this Award.

2   That one day after the delivery of the signed Award the Building Owner shall be at liberty if they chose but shall be under no obligation to carry out the following works.

(b)   **[insert description of proposed works]**

3   That no material deviation from the agreed works shall be made without prior consultation with and agreement by the agreed Surveyor.

4   That if the Building Owners exercise the above rights they shall:

(b)   Execute the whole of the aforesaid works at the sole cost of the building Owner.

(c)   Take all reasonable precautions and provide all necessary support to retain the Adjoining Owners land and buildings.

(d)   Make good all structural or decorative damage to the Adjoining Owners building occasioned by the said works in materials to match existing works to the satisfaction of the appointed Surveyors, or if so required by the Adjoining Owner make payment in lieu of carrying out the work to make the damage good.

(e) Hold the Adjoining Owner free from liability for any injury or loss of life to any person or damage to property caused by, or in consequence of, the execution of said works.

(f) Bear the costs of the making of any justified claims.

(g) Permit the **Agreed Surveyor** to have access to both the Building Owner(s) and Adjoining Owner(s)   premises at all reasonable times during the progress of the said works.

(h) Carry out the whole of the said works so far as practical from the Building Owners' side. Where access to the Adjoining Owner's premises is required reasonable notice shall be given in accordance with Section 8 of the Act.

(i) Remove any scaffolding or screens as soon as possible and clear away dust and debris from time to time as necessary.

(j) All **NOISY** works to be restricted between the hours of 7.30am and 5.30pm weekdays and 8.00am and 12.30pm Saturdays.

(k) Shall not block right of way of Adjoining Owners garden entrances.

(l) Clean down and remove any debris, dirt and or dust daily/ weekly/monthly from the adjoining owners property.

(m) Any variation from the proposed drawings referred to above must be bought to the attention of the appointed party wall surveyor, for his consideration of any variations accordingly.

(n) Will not deposit any materials on Adjoining Owners property without consent of the Agreed Surveyor.

(o) Shall take all necessary precautions and cover all excavations at the end of working day.

5   That the whole of the works referred to in this Award shall be executed in accordance with Building Regulations, and any other requirements of statutory authorities, and shall be executed in a proper and workmanlike manner in sound and suitable materials in accordance with the terms of this Award to the reasonable satisfaction of the **Agreed Surveyor.**

6   That the works shall be carried through with reasonable expedition after commencement and so as to avoid any unnecessary inconvenience to the Adjoining Owner(s) or occupier(s).

7   That the signed Awards shall be served upon the Appointing Owner(s) forthwith, and the building owner(s) shall notify their contractor of the awards contents, obligations and duties where relevant.

8   That upon the signing of this Award the Building Owners will pay the Agreed Surveyors fee of £ **[insert fee]** plus VAT in connection with the preparation of this Award and including one final inspection. In the event of damage being caused or other contingencies or variations arising, including the pursuing of any sums owed in pursuance of the Act, a further fee shall be payable calculated on an hourly rate of £ **[insert rate]** exclusive of VAT and disbursements.

9   Any costs incurred by either party in settling any matter shall be discussed in accordance with Section 10(13)(a)(b)(c) at the rate so awarded.

10   That the **Agreed Surveyor** reserves the right to make and issue any further Award or Awards that may be necessary, as provided in said Act.

11   That this Award shall be null and void if the permitted works do not commence within 12 months from the date of the notices.

12   Noting in this Award shall be held as conferring, admitting or affecting any right of light or air, or any other easement.

IN WITNESS WHEREOF I **[insert surveyors name and address]** have set my hands this [insert date]

Agreed Surveyor to the leave:

Witness:

Occupation:

Address:

23.8 Appointed Award

AN AWARD under the provisions
Of the PARTY WALL etc ACT,
1996 to be served on the
Appointing Owners under Section 10(14)

WHEREAS **[insert Building Owner(s) name(s)** (hereinafter referred to as the Building Owner) of **[insert address]** freehold owners within the meaning of the said Act of the premises known as **[insert address]** did on the **[insert date of notice]** serve upon **[insert Adjoining Owner(s) name(s)** (hereinafter referred to as the Adjoining Owner) freehold owner within the meaning of the Act of the adjoining premises known as **[insert Adjoining Owners address]** notice of their intention to exercise the rights given to them by the Party Wall etc Act 1996 under **[insert details of notices served]**

AND WHEREAS A DISPUTE HAS ARISEN the Building Owner has appointed **[insert surveyors details]** to act as the **Building Owners Surveyor** and the Adjoining Owners have appointed **[insert surveyors details],** to act as their surveyor.

AND WHEREAS they have selected **[insert Third Surveyors name and address]** to act as **Third Surveyor** in accordance with the provisions of the Party Wall etc., Act and, in the event of his being unable or unwilling to act and there being unable jointly to agree upon a substitute, they have agreed that another third surveyor shall be appointed in accordance with Section 10(8) of the said Act.

NOW WE, being the **Two Surveyors** so appointed, having inspected the said premises DO HEREBY AWARD AND DETERMINE as follows:—

1. a)   That the **wall separating** the building owners and adjoining owners premises is deemed to be a party wall within the meaning of the Act.

    (f)   That the Adjoining Owners' building stands close to the Building Owners' premises within the meaning of the Act.

    (g)   That the Schedule of Condition dated **2ⁿᵈ May 2008** attached hereto and signed by the said **The Two Surveyors** forms part of this Award.

    (h)   That the attached Schedule of Condition is sufficient for the present purposes of the this Award.

    (i)   That Drawings Nos**. [insert drawing details]** and attached hereto and any others which may become relevant and signed by us the Said two Surveyors form part of this Award.

2   That **fourteen days** after the service of the signed Award the Building Owner shall be at liberty if they choose but shall be under no obligation to carry out the following works.

    (b)   Will not deposit any materials on Adjoining Owners property without consent of the Appointed Surveyors.

    (c)   Excavate foundations to a depth of 1.0m below ground level and mass fill with concrete.

    (d)   To provide protective membrane covering to the full area of the adjoining owner's path adjacent to the flank wall and provide 18mm plywood sheeting for the duration of the project.

    (e)   Erect tubular scaffolding as necessary to execute the works to construct the proposed extension.

    (f)   Remove all builders' materials, debris and tools at the end of each working day.

    (g)   On completion of the works remove all protective coverings, scaffolding, materials and wash down and clean all surfaces of patio and path to the satisfaction of the appointed surveyors.

3   That no material deviation from the agreed works shall be made without prior consultation with and agreement by the said two Surveyor's.

4   That if the Building Owner exercises the above rights they shall;

(o)   Execute the whole of the aforesaid works at the sole cost of the Building Owner.

(p)   Take all reasonable precautions and provide all necessary support to protect the Adjoining Owner's land and buildings.

(q)   Make good all structural or decorative damage to the Adjoining Owner's building occasioned by the said works in materials to match existing works to the satisfaction of the Appointed Surveyor's, or if so required by the Adjoining Owner make payment in lieu of carrying out the work to make the damage good.

(r)   Shall take all necessary precautions and cover all excavations at the end of working day and provide security fencing to all boundaries where walls/fences have been removed.

(s)   Hold the Adjoining Owner free from liability for any injury or loss of life to any person or damage to property caused by, or in consequence of, the execution of said works.

(t)   Bear the reasonable costs of the making of any justified claims.

(u)   Permit the Adjoining Owner's Surveyor to have access to the Building Owners' premises at all reasonable times during the progress of the said works.

(v)   Carry out the whole of the said works so far as practical from the Building Owner's. Where access to the Adjoining Owner's premises is required reasonable notice shall be given in accordance with Section 8 of the Act.

(w)   All noisy works to be restricted between the hours of 7.30 am and 5.30 pm weekdays and 8.00 am and 12.30 pm Saturdays.

(x)   And will take all reasonable care to protect the Adjoining Owners property and reinstate all disturbed areas

5   That the **Building Owners Surveyor** shall be permitted access
to the Adjoining Owner's property from time to time during the
progress of the works at reasonable times and after giving twenty
four hours written notice.

6   That the whole of the works referred to in this Award shall be
executed in accordance with Building Regulations, and any other
requirements of statutory authorities, and shall be executed in a
proper and workmanlike manner in sound and suitable materials
in accordance with the terms of this Award to the reasonable
satisfaction of the two said Surveyors.

7   That the works shall be carried through with reasonable expedition
after commencement and so as to avoid any unnecessary
inconvenience to the Adjoining Owners or occupiers. In particular
noisy works the subject of this Award shall be restricted to between
the hours of 8.00am and 17.00pm.

8   That the signed Awards shall be delivered to the Appointing Owners
forthwith and an unsigned copy provided to the adjoining owners
surveyor and the Building Owners contractor, who shall be made
aware of its contents

9   That upon the signing of this Award the Building Owners will pay
the Building Owners Surveyors fee of £**[insert fees]** plus VAT in
connection with the preparation of this Award and including one
final inspection. In the event of damage being caused or other
contingencies or variations arising, including the pursuing of any
sums owed in pursuance of the Act, a further fee shall be payable

calculated on an hourly rate of £ **[insert rate]** exclusive of VAT and disbursements.

10   That upon the signing of this Award the Building Owners will pay the Adjoining Owners Surveyors fee of £ **[insert fees]** plus VAT in connection with the preparation of this Award and including one final inspection. In the event of damage being caused or other contingencies or variations arising, including the pursuing of any sums owed in pursuance of the Act, a further fee shall be payable calculated on an hourly rate of £ **[insert rate]** exclusive of VAT and disbursements.

11   Any costs incurred by either party in settling this matter shall be discussed and agreed in accordance with Section 10(13)(a)(b)(c) at the agreed rate.

12   That the Appointed Surveyors reserve the right to make and issue any further Award or Awards that may be necessary, as provided in said Act.

13   That this Award shall be null and void if the permitted works do not commence within 12 months from the date of the Notice(s).

14   Nothing in this Award shall be held as conferring, admitting or affecting any right of light or air.

15   That nothing in this Award shall be held as inferring, transferring or ascribing any responsibility to any of the three said Surveyors in regard to Health and Safety matters and particularly in relation to the Construction (Design and Management) Regulations 2007 (if applicable).

IN WITNESS WHEREOF We have set our hands this .... day of ....

[insert surveyors name]

Appointed Surveyor to the Building Owner:

Witness:

Occupation:

Address:

Appointed Surveyor to the Adjoining Owner:

Witness:

Occupation:

Address:

23.9 Service of an Award Letter

Date: **[insert date]**
Your Ref:
Our Ref:

[insert address]

Dear **[insert name(s)],**

Re: Party Wall Etc., Act 1996
[insert address]

I am pleased to serve the Party Wall Award made and signed by the appointed Surveyors, which sets out the owner's rights and duties in connection with the proposed works.

I would advise that pursuant to the Act Section 10 (17) as an Owner(s) you are legally entitled to appeal the Award within 14 days through the County Court if you consider this award is invalid or unreasonable for whatever reason.

"Section 10 (17) either of the parties to the dispute may, within the period of 14 days beginning with the date on which an Award made under this section is served on him, appeal to the County Court against the Award and the County Court may":

a)   *Rescind the Award or modify it in such manner as the Court thinks fit;*
b)   *Make such order as to costs as the Court thinks fit.*

Please note that the fourteen day period cannot be extended and you must therefore seek independent legal advice if you have any concerns in respect of the award.

However, in my opinion and to the best of my knowledge, I believe that there is nothing within the Award, which would justify this course of action.

I enclose a second copy of the Award that should be given to your contractors.

I trust the foregoing is satisfactory.

Yours sincerely,

23.10 Security of expenses letter

Adjoining Owner(s) Name   Building owner(s) Name
Address   Address

Dear

Re: The Party Wall etc. Act 1996
   Matters at (BO property address & AO property address)

I apologise for the formality of this letter but there are certain rights under the Act which I am obliged to advise you of.

The adjoining owner(s) are entitled under section 12(1) to serve a notice requesting security of expenses as may be agreed between **[insert AOS and BOS name]**. If an agreement cannot be reached on the amount of reasonable security then the appointed surveyors will determine an appropriate sum under section 10 of the Act.

s.12(1)   An adjoining owner may serve a notice requiring the building owner before he begins any work in the exercise of the rights conferred by this Act to give such security as may be agreed between the owners or in the event of dispute determined in accordance with section 10.

If you intend to request security of expenses please provide your request in writing. However should you require any further clarification on any points please do not hesitate to contact me.

Yours sincerely,

23.11 Referral to Third Surveyor

Adjoining Owner(s) Name   Building owner(s) Name
Address   Address

Dear

Re: The Party Wall etc. Act 1996
Matters at (BO property address & AO property address)

I apologise for the formality of this letter but there are certain rights which I am obliged to advise you of.

Following dissent to the notices the appointed surveyor(s) under s.10(1) (b) are required to forthwith agree the selection of a third surveyor. I can confirm that we have therefore selected;

Name
Address
Tel no

Accordingly, under s.10(11) of the Act, (a copy of which is produced below for clarification) allows either of the owner(s) or the surveyor(s) to call upon the third surveyor to determine any disputed matters.

s.10(11)   Either of the parties or either of the surveyors appointed by the parties may call upon the third surveyor selected in pursuant of this section to determine the disputed matters and he shall make the necessary award

If you have any concerns about the conduct of the surveyors or the party wall matters in any way, I would sincerely hope that you would contact me in the first instance so that we could try and resolve any concerns you have. However, you are entitled at your discretion to refer any matter to the third surveyor.

I trust the foregoing is satisfactory.

Yours sincerely,

23.12 Special Foundations Letter

Adjoining Owner(s) Name
Address

Dear **[insert Building owner(s) name]**

Re: The Party Wall etc. Act 1996
Request for special foundations to be positioned on the Adjoining Owners property [AO property address]

Further to your request under section 7(4) to place special foundations onto my land as detailed in the drawings attached to the notices served on **[insert date of notices]**. I hereby **(consent/dissent)** and understand that my appointed surveyor will deal with the issues arising from the **special foundations and or alternative foundations** within the Award.

We trust the foregoing clarifies our position.

Yours sincerely,

cc: **Building Owner(s) Surveyor**
  Adjoining Owner(s) Surveyor

23.13 Informing the Third Surveyor

Address

Dear Sir,

· **Re: The Party Wall etc. Act 1996**
[insert Adjoining Owners and Building Owners names and addresses]

In respect of the above matter and having been appointed as the **[Building Owner(s) Surveyor/Adjoining Owner(s) Surveyor [delete as appropriate] I** am pleased to advise that you have been selected as the Third Surveyor. I enclose copies of your formal selection in writing and confirm that there is no dispute for you to determine at present. This letter is to enquire whether you are (i) prepared to accept the selection and (ii) ask you to confirm that there is no conflict of interest with any of the parties related to this matter.

If you have any questions may I respectfully ask that you raise those questions in writing and provide a copy simultaneously to both myself and my opposite surveyor.

I trust the foregoing is satisfactory and hopefully your services in this matter will not be required. As soon as you have confirmed you are wiling to accept the selection I will advise my Appointing Owner(s) of their rights under section 10(11).

Yours sincerely,

23.14 Checklist

1) Receipt of notices check validity
2) Establish identity of owners, land registry checks, and obtain letter of appointment
3) Exchange letters of appointment with opposite surveyor
4) Agree the selection of the Third Surveyor
5) Notify the Appointing Owner(s) of the Third Surveyors identity and contact details
6) Raise any initial observations (if special foundations are involved) explain procedures to Adjoining Owner(s) and seek written consent or dissent
7) Notify Adjoining Owner(s) of provision of security of expenses under section 12(1)
8) Arrange (if possible) access to prepare a schedule of condition
9) Prepare a draft award and agree content of award
10) Serve award and advise on rights of appeal
11) Deal with issues as a consequence of the works
12) On completion of works carry out a final inspection, if no damage is caused send final completion letter to opposite surveyor
13) If damage has been caused deal with damage in accordance with the procedures of the Act

15637439R00148

Printed in Great Britain
by Amazon